Approaches to Highly Parameterized Inversion: Pilot-Point Theory, Guidelines, and Research Directions

By John E. Doherty, Michael N. Fienen and Randall J. Hunt

Scientific Investigations Report 2010–5168

U.S. Department of the Interior
U.S. Geological Survey

U.S. Department of the Interior
KEN SALAZAR, Secretary

U.S. Geological Survey
Marcia K. McNutt, Director

U.S. Geological Survey, Reston, Virginia: 2010

For more information on the USGS—the Federal source for science about the Earth, its natural and living resources, natural hazards, and the environment, visit http://www.usgs.gov or call 1-888-ASK-USGS

For an overview of USGS information products, including maps, imagery, and publications, visit http://www.usgs.gov/pubprod

To order this and other USGS information products, visit http://store.usgs.gov

Suggested citation:
Doherty, J.E., Fienen, M.N., and Hunt, R.J., 2010, Approaches to highly parameterized inversion: Pilot-point theory, guidelines, and research directions: U.S. Geological Survey Scientific Investigations Report 2010–5168, 36 p.

Contents

Contents—Continued

Figures

Approaches to Highly Parameterized Inversion: Pilot-Point Theory, Guidelines, and Research Directions

By John E. Doherty[1,2], Michael N. Fienen[3], and Randall J. Hunt[3]

Abstract

Pilot points have been used in geophysics and hydrogeology for at least 30 years as a means to bridge the gap between estimating a parameter value in every cell of a model and subdividing models into a small number of homogeneous zones. Pilot points serve as surrogate parameters at which values are estimated in the inverse-modeling process, and their values are interpolated onto the modeling domain in such a way that heterogeneity can be represented at a much lower computational cost than trying to estimate parameters in every cell of a model. Although the use of pilot points is increasingly common, there are few works documenting the mathematical implications of their use and even fewer sources of guidelines for their implementation in hydrogeologic modeling studies. This report describes the mathematics of pilot-point use, provides guidelines for their use in the parameter-estimation software suite (PEST), and outlines several research directions. Two key attributes for pilot-point definitions are highlighted. First, the difference between the information contained in the every-cell parameter field and the surrogate parameter field created using pilot points should be in the realm of parameters which are not informed by the observed data (the null space). Second, the interpolation scheme for projecting pilot-point values onto model cells ideally should be orthogonal. These attributes are informed by the mathematics and have important ramifications for both the guidelines and suggestions for future research.

Introduction

Pilot Points and Groundwater-Model Calibration

The use of pilot points as a spatial parameterization device in groundwater-model calibration is becoming commonplace. Pilot points can be useful for any model parameter or boundary condition, but are most commonly applied to aquifer hydraulic conductivity. Early uses include those of de Marsily and others (1984), Certes and de Marsily (1991), and LaVenue and Pickens (1992) and were extended by RamaRao and others (1995), LaVenue and others (1995), and LaVenue and de Marsily (2001). The latter authors combined the use of pilot points with a methodology for optimal selection of pilot-point locations. They also developed a methodology for using pilot points in conjunction with stochastic fields to derive multiple hydraulic-property distributions that on one hand calibrate a model, while on the other hand respect the geostatistical characterization of a study area. Use of multiple field realizations in making model predictions allows the exploration of estimates of the uncertainty associated with these predictions. Kowalsky and others (2004) implemented a pilot-point formulation for use with a maximum a posteriori (MAP) likelihood method for hydrogeophysical applications.

Doherty (2003) used pilot points in the context of underdetermined model calibration. Underdetermined problems are those where the number of parameters exceeds that which can be uniquely estimated based on a given observation dataset, a common occurrence in the highly parameterized problems such as those motivating the use of pilot points. In such problems, uniqueness in solution of the inverse problem is achieved through the use of mathematical regularization. Regularization is a general class of methods that provides stability and uniqueness to calibrating underdetermined models by adding constraints of structure or a preferred condition to the parameters being estimated (see, for example, Hunt and others 2007). While regularization is a necessary component of this extension of pilot points to underdetermined problems, regularization has been used in many other contexts for a much longer time (see, for example, Tikhonov and Arsenin, 1977 and Tarantola, 2005). For general information about regularization, Menke (1984) and Aster and others (2005) provide introductory discussions.

The use of pilot points in an underdetermined context marked a departure from conventional pilot-point usage in that the restriction of greatly limiting the number of parameters could be relaxed, allowing pilot points to be distributed liberally throughout a model domain. Parsimony is achieved by restricting the infinite possible number of solutions in

[1] Watermark Numerical Computing, Brisbane, Australia.

[2] National Centre for Groundwater Research and Training, Flinders University, Adelaide SA, Australia.

[3] U.S. Geological Survey.

an underdetermined problem only to include solutions (1) reflecting the level of complexity in the underlying parameter field that is supported by the data, and (2) that are consistent with the general (soft) knowledge of the site. Documentation of their use as an adjunct to underdetermined parameter estimation continued with Tonkin and Doherty (2005) who used the hybrid subspace—Tikhonov "singular value decomposition (SVD)—assist" scheme provided by the PEST parameter-estimation software (Doherty, 2010; Doherby and Hunt, 2010) as a means of efficient mitigation of the large computational burden incurred in highly parameterized problems. Alcolea and others (2006, 2008) also have used pilot points as a parameterization device in the regularized inversion setting, both in model calibration, and in constraining stochastic fields to respect calibration constraints while conducting parameter and predictive uncertainty analysis. Using a synthetic model, Christensen and Doherty (2008) explored the effects of pilot point spacing and interpolation methods on model predictive accuracy.

The use of many pilot points in regularized inversion contexts has led to the development of new methodologies for exploration of calibration-constrained model predictive uncertainty analysis. Such an analysis only is representative when it accounts for both solution space and null space contributions to parameter and predictive uncertainty (Moore and Doherty, 2005, 2006; Doherty, Hunt, and Tonkin, 2010). The solution space is the portion of parameter space that is informed by the observations while the null space accounts for parameters (or combinations of parameters) that are unknown and not informed by observations. Use of a large number of pilot points as a basis for model parameterization allows the null space contribution to predictive error/uncertainty to be at least partially explored (see Hunt and Doherty, 2006; Doherty, Hunt, and Tonkin, 2010). Model predictive uncertainty analysis in conjunction with pilot-point parameterization was demonstrated by Tonkin and others (2007) who used a constrained maximization/minimization process to compute predictive confidence limits. Their use, in conjunction with stochastic field generation, in conducting highly efficient calibration-constrained Monte Carlo analysis was explored by Tonkin and Doherty (2009). Gallagher and Doherty (2007) demonstrated their use in linear uncertainty analysis. Not only can the uncertainty of key model predictions be estimated through such an analysis, but contributions to that uncertainty by different parameter groups also can be determined. The efficacy of different observation types in reducing that uncertainty also can be established.

Implementation of Pilot-Point Parameterization

Support for pilot-point parameterization in the MODFLOW/MT3DMS context is provided by many groundwater model commercial graphical-user interfaces.

In addition, the PEST Groundwater Data Utilities (Doherty, 2007) support use of pilot points in conjunction with the MODFLOW (Harbaugh, 2005), MT3DMS (Zheng, 1990), SEAWAT (Langevin and others, 2008), FEFLOW (Diersch, 2009), MicroFEM (Hemker and de Boer, 2009), and RSM (South Florida Water Management District, 2005) groundwater models. In the MODFLOW/MT3DMS/SEAWAT context, functionality provided by these utilities supports pilot-point parameterization on a layer-by-layer basis and on a hydrostratigraphic unit-by-unit basis; a hydrostratigraphic unit can encompass (and/or intersect) many different model layers. In all cases, pilot points are assumed to be distributed on a two-dimensional areal basis; however, horizontal interpolation between pilot points can be combined with vertical interpolation between model layers to realize a pseudo-three-dimensional pilot-point-based interpolation scheme for parameterization of multi-layered hydrostratigraphic units. Throughout this report, we refer to the finest discretization of parameter values as occurring on a "cell" and "grid" basis, implying use with a finite-difference or finite-volume model. The methods and findings could also be applied to a finite-element model, in which case the finest discretization would be on an "element" basis.

In addition to providing the means to undertake spatial interpolation from pilot points to the cells of a numerical groundwater model, software provided with the PEST Groundwater Data Utilities suite provides the means to add prior information equations to a PEST input dataset applying regularization and to add soft-knowledge constraints to a pilot-point parameter set. A number of options are supported, implementing both inter- and intra-hydrostratigraphic unit parameter constraints.

Purpose and Scope

Despite the fact that pilot-point-based parameterization of groundwater models is now commonplace, their use in model calibration is largely ad hoc, with implementation guided by intuition rather than mathematics. The mathematical analysis of the use of pilot points in groundwater-model calibration has been the subject of little research. The costs and benefits of their use have therefore not been quantified, nor have mathematically backed guidelines for their use been documented. As a result, a basis has not been created for further research into their usage that can result in improved efficiency and performance of pilot-point-based calibration or identify contexts where their usage may be problematic.

The purpose of this report is to address these shortcomings by (1) presenting and reviewing the theoretical underpinning for the use of pilot points, (2) providing implementation guidelines based on this theory, and (3) providing suggestions for further research and development to improve pilot-point usage in groundwater-model calibration.

Conceptual Overview of Pilot-Point Usage

The goal of pilot points is to provide an intermediate approach for characterizing heterogeneity in groundwater models between direct representation of cell-by-cell variability and reduction of parameterization to few homogeneous zones. Figure 1 depicts a schematic representation of the process of using pilot-points. In figure 1A, a heterogeneous field is depicted overlain by a model grid. This illustrates that, even at the model-cell scale, the representation of heterogeneity requires simplification as each model cell must be assigned a single value representative of the entire area that it overlies. In figure 1B, a network of pilot-points is shown in which the size of the circle is proportional to the parameter value, and the color represents the value on the same color scale as in figure 1A. The general pattern of variability in the true field is visible in this image, but the resolution is much coarser than reality. Figure 1C shows the pilot-point values interpolated onto a very fine grid and illustrates that much of the true heterogeneity can be reconstructed from a subset of sampled values provided that appropriate interpolation is performed. Figure 1d shows the interpolated version of the pilot-point values in figure 1B on the model-cell grid scale, which represents the version of reality that the model would actually reflect.

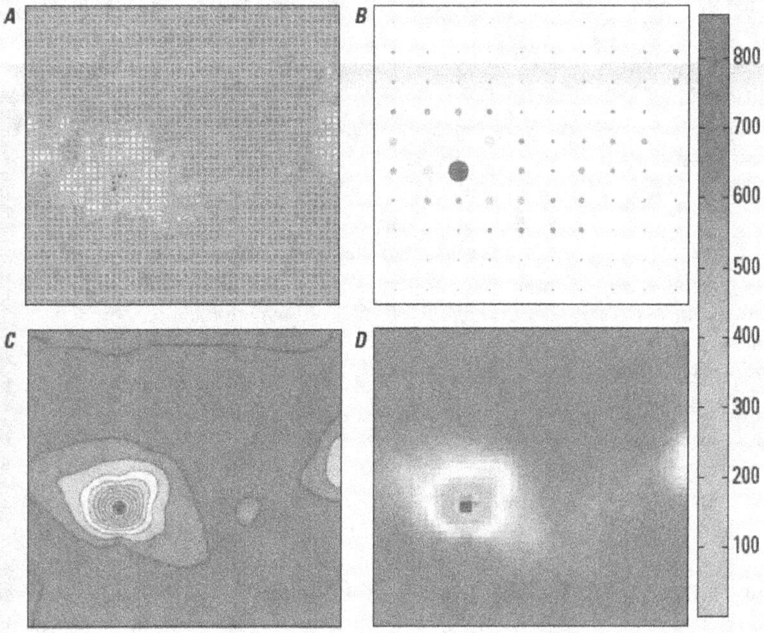

Figure 1. Conceptual overview of representing complex hydrogeologic conditions using pilot points. Panel (*A*) shows the inherent property value overlain by the model grid in gray. Panel (*B*) is a representation of the true property values by a grid of pilot points in which symbol size indicates value. Panel (*C*) shows an interpolated representation of panel (*B*) on an arbitrarily fine grid scale. Panel (*D*) shows the value from the pilot points interpolated to the computational-grid scale. Interpolation in all cases was performed using ordinary Kriging. The same color scale, in arbitrary units, applies to all four panels.

The approach taken in this report to model calibration is based on regularized inversion discussed by Hunt and others (2007), whereby many parameters are represented in a model, and that solution of the inverse problem (the problem of model calibration) is undertaken using mathematical regularization as a stabilization device and means of obtaining a unique solution. The benefits of this approach to model calibration are discussed by Hunt and others (2007) and briefly discussed in later sections of this report.

Conceptually, every cell of a numerical model can be assigned a different set of parameters. In fact, real-world hydraulic properties show so much spatial variability that if a model were to provide an accurate representation of hydraulic properties and processes throughout its domain, a very fine grid discretization would be needed, and the properties assigned to each cell would be different. However, there is an upper limit to the parameterization detail that can be inferred from a given calibration dataset. Therefore, any "calibrated model" is capable of representing only broad-scale aspects of parameterization spatial variability, with greater potential for representation of this variability where data density is greater and comparatively error-free. Nevertheless, where a large number of parameters are included in the calibration process, and where parameter simplification is achieved through mathematical means, this simplification can be implemented such that maximum information is extracted from a given calibration dataset by endowing the calibration process with the flexibility it needs to emplace heterogeneity where it needs to be placed, while subduing representation of spurious heterogeneity or geometric artificialities (such as boundaries between zones of assumed piecewise constancy) that are not supported by the calibration dataset.

Mathematically, there is no limit to the number of parameters that can be used in the regularized inversion process; however, in most contexts of groundwater-model calibration an upper limit is set by the computational burden of having to compute derivatives of model outputs with respect to adjustable parameters. Therefore, a "reduced parameter set" must be developed that, of necessity, requires some kind of "lumping" or "averaging" of hydraulic properties as represented on a cell-by-cell basis in the numerical model.

The notion of regularization is implicit in the use of a reduced parameter set, for it is a form of parameter simplification that eradicates the possibility of certain scales of hydraulic property variability from appearing in the calibrated model. As a result, this detail is not available to confound the parameter-estimation process. When (mathematical) regularized inversion also is applied to the reduced parameter set, two forms of regularization are active: implicit regularization arising from parameter reduction and explicit regularization specified through mathematical calibration algorithms. An immediate challenge is to ensure that regularization implicit in using a reduced parameter set does not erode the benefits provided by the explicit mathematical regularization used to solve the inverse problem, or if it does, to ensure that the degradation is minimal.

Use of a reduced parameter set often requires manual intervention and (or) subjective decision-making by the modeler. Ideally, these decisions should be as informed as possible. Where pilot points are used for parameter reduction, decisions need to be made on the locations and density of placement of these points, on the manner in which spatial interpolation is conducted between them and the model grid, and on the type of mathematical regularization applied to the reduced parameter set. Although it is possible (and perhaps desirable) that the entire process be automated, design of a pilot-point parameterization scheme is currently (2010) implemented by mostly manual means; however, whether it is implemented automatically or manually, design of such a scheme should be informed by the knowledge of the regularization role of pilot points and of the way in which this regularization interacts with the mathematical regularization used to constrain the calibration process. This report is an attempt to provide the foundation for such awareness.

Theory

Let the vector **k** represent the hydraulic properties of a simulated system at the level at which they can be represented in a model: the grid scale. Although parameters will not normally be represented with this level of detail during the calibration process (because of the extremely high dimensionality of **k**), it is necessary to consider parameterization at this level of detail to begin, because heterogeneity within the real world exists at this scale (and probably at a finer scale). Such a conceptualization represents "reality" (as far as it can be represented in the model). Consideration of parameterization at the finest representable scale allows us to develop a theoretical description of the compromises that are made in representing it at the coarser scale required for numerical convenience during the model-calibration process.

Suppose further that the model is linear with respect to its parameters, so the relation between model parameters and model outputs can be represented by a matrix operator. We designate the matrix that represents the relation between model parameters and those model outputs that correspond to measurements comprising the calibration dataset as **Z**.

Let **h** be a vector that represents historical observations of system state that comprise the calibration dataset. Then (ignoring parameter and observation offsets for convenience)

$$\mathbf{h} = \mathbf{Zk} + \varepsilon\,, \tag{1}$$

where ε represents epistemic uncertainty, including noise associated with the measurements and errors arising from model inadequacies, which, in this document, we will refer to as "structural noise."

It is presumed that unique estimation of **k** from **h** is impossible owing to the number of elements comprising the vector **k**, and the limited information content (and number of elements) contained within the calibration dataset **h**. Thus, **Z** has a null space, meaning there exist vectors δ**k** for which

$$\mathbf{Z}\delta\mathbf{k} = \mathbf{0}\,. \tag{2}$$

Conceptually, the fact that **Z** has a null space means that there are values of **k** that, even if they vary substantially, will not affect the calculation of model outputs that correspond to **h** in equation 1. This is profound because if certain parameters cannot affect these outputs, they are inestimable based on **h**.

For convenience, let it be assumed that

1. The model is a perfect simulator of environmental behavior, and

2. There is no noise associated with historical measurements of system state.

Equation 1 then becomes

$$\mathbf{h} = \mathbf{Zk}\,. \tag{3}$$

Notwithstanding the fact that observation datasets on whose basis parameter estimation takes place are always contaminated by measurement (and structural) noise, initial consideration of a noise-free dataset allows insights into the effect that estimation of a "lumped," "reduced," or "averaged" parameter set as an intermediary step in estimation of **k**, actually has on the estimates of **k** so obtained.

Generalized Inverse

There are many (infinite) equations that satisfy equation 3, because of equation 2. In seeking any **k** that satisfies equation 3, we are in fact seeking a generalized inverse of **Z**, designated as $\mathbf{Z}^{-}$.

The generalized inverse ($\mathbf{A}^{-}$) of a rank-deficient matrix (**A**) is defined through the relation

$$\mathbf{A} = \mathbf{A}\mathbf{A}^{-}\mathbf{A}\,. \tag{4}$$

When applied to our model encapsulated in the matrix **Z**, this implies that we seek a parameter set $\underline{\mathbf{k}}$ that allows us to reproduce the heads **h** through the relation

$$\underline{\mathbf{k}} = \mathbf{Z}^{-}\mathbf{h}\,. \tag{5}$$

Because there is a plethora of vectors **k** that satisfy equation 3, there also is a plethora of generalized inverses $\mathbf{Z}^{-}$ of **Z**. One of these, however, the so-called Moore-Penrose pseudoinverse (Moore, 1920 and Penrose, 1955), is especially significant because it is unique, and it leads to a minimum norm solution for $\underline{\mathbf{k}}$.

The Moore-Penrose pseudoinverse $\mathbf{A}^{+}$ of the matrix **A** has the following properties (Koch, 1987)

$$\mathbf{A}\mathbf{A}^{+}\mathbf{A} = \mathbf{A} \tag{6a}$$

$$\mathbf{A}^{+}\mathbf{A}\mathbf{A}^{+} = \mathbf{A}^{+} \tag{6b}$$

$$(\mathbf{A}\mathbf{A}^{+})^{T} = \mathbf{A}\mathbf{A}^{+} \tag{6c}$$

$$(\mathbf{A}^{+}\mathbf{A})^{T} = \mathbf{A}^{+}\mathbf{A} \tag{6d}$$

where $(\,)^{T}$ indicates a matrix transpose.

Note that equation 6d is equivalent to insisting that the resolution matrix obtained as a by-product of solution of the ill-posed inverse problem is symmetric. For a full discussion of the resolution matrix see, for example, Menke (1984), Aster and others (2005), and Moore and Doherty (2005). As discussed in these and other references, the resolution matrix, defined as $\mathbf{A}^{+}\mathbf{A}$ in the current context, has the notable property that each of its rows represents the "averaging coefficients" through which the simplified parameters as represented in a model are derived from their real-world counterparts. At the extreme of $\mathbf{A}^{+}\mathbf{A}$ being equal to an identity matrix, no averaging takes place and the estimate of **k** is perfect. In practice, this extreme can never be achieved so the resolution matrix represents the blurring, or simplification, of reality required to achieve a unique solution of the inverse problem.

Let C(**k**) denote the covariance matrix of **k**. This is a matrix that describes the innate variability of **k**, including the degree of spatial correlation that exists between parameters of the same type at different locations within the model domain, and between parameters of different types at the same or different locations. It can thus be considered to be a result of geological site characterization. In a small number of cases it can be the outcome of a comprehensive geostatistical study; more often, it is simply an expression of the fact that quantitative geological knowledge is limited but not absent.

Suppose that C(**k**) can be represented by the relation

$$C(\mathbf{k}) = \sigma_k^2\mathbf{I}\,, \tag{7}$$

where **I** is the identity matrix and σ_k^2 is variance (note that this condition implies stationarity of **k**). In this case, the minimum norm solution for $\underline{\mathbf{k}}$ corresponds to the solution of maximum likelihood for $\underline{\mathbf{k}}$ (if it is normally distributed). This solution is not actually "likely," but it is a simplified solution about which potential parametric error is roughly symmetric. Symmetry of potential error indicates that the solution is unbiased. Ideally, the same applies to model predictions made based on the estimated parameter set $\underline{\mathbf{k}}$.

The Moore-Penrose pseudoinverse is computed easily through singular value decomposition (SVD) of the matrix **Z**. Through SVD,

$$\mathbf{Z} = \mathbf{U}\mathbf{S}\mathbf{V}^{T}\,, \tag{8}$$

where **U** is a matrix composed of orthogonal unit vectors spanning the range space of **Z**, **V** is a matrix of orthogonal unit vectors spanning the domain of **Z** (therefore parameter space), **S** is a matrix of singular values whose off-diagonal elements are zero. Equation 8 can be re-written as

$$\mathbf{Z} = \mathbf{U}\begin{bmatrix}\mathbf{S}_1 & \mathbf{S}_2\end{bmatrix}\begin{bmatrix}\mathbf{V}_1^{T}\\ \mathbf{V}_2^{T}\end{bmatrix}, \tag{9}$$

where $\mathbf{S}_2$ is **0** and $\mathbf{S}_1$ contains only non-zero singular values of **Z**. The vectors comprising the columns of $\mathbf{V}_1$ span the solution space of the matrix **Z**, while those comprising the columns of $\mathbf{V}_2$ span its null space. From equation 9,

$$\mathbf{Z} = \mathbf{U}\mathbf{S}_1\mathbf{V}_1^{T} + \mathbf{U}\mathbf{S}_2\mathbf{V}_1^{T} = \mathbf{U}\mathbf{S}_1\mathbf{V}_1^{T}\,. \tag{10}$$

Through substitution of equation 10 into equation 3, we readily obtain for $\underline{\mathbf{k}}$,

$$\underline{\mathbf{k}} = \mathbf{V}_1\mathbf{V}_1^{T}\mathbf{k} = \mathbf{V}_1\mathbf{S}_1^{-1}\mathbf{U}^{T}\mathbf{h}\,, \tag{11}$$

from which it is apparent that the Moore-Penrose pseudoinverse of **Z** is

$$\mathbf{Z}^{+} = \mathbf{V}_1\mathbf{S}_1^{-1}\mathbf{U}^{T} \tag{12}$$

Equation 11 reveals that the inferred or "calibrated" parameter field $\underline{\mathbf{k}}$ is the projection of the real-world parameter field **k** onto the solution space of **Z**. In practice, however, the dimensions of the solution space are reduced by relegation of columns of $\mathbf{V}_1$ associated with small singular values to the calibration null space, this being done to minimize contamination of the estimated parameter field $\underline{\mathbf{k}}$ by measurement noise. See Moore and Doherty (2005) for more details.

Albert (1972, p. 19) shows that the Moore-Penrose pseudoinverse of the matrix **A** also can be expressed as

$$\mathbf{A}^{+} = \lim_{\delta \to 0} \left[\mathbf{A}^{T}\mathbf{A} + \delta^{2}\mathbf{I}\right]^{-1}\mathbf{A}^{T} = \lim_{\delta \to 0} \mathbf{A}^{T}\left[\mathbf{A}\mathbf{A}^{T} + \delta^{2}\mathbf{I}\right]^{-1}. \quad (13)$$

We will make use of this important result later.

Reduced Parameters

In this and the following subsections, the concept of a reduced parameter set is introduced. This is defined as a smaller set of parameters used in the calibration process than those represented by the detailed parameter set **k**. The reduced parameter set is used as a practical replacement for the **k** parameter set and may be composed of any combination of values assigned to pilot points, zones of piecewise constancy, and (or) parameters defined based on any other parameterization device.

Replacing the detailed parameter set represented by **k** with a reduced parameter set, and estimating values for the latter during the calibration process as an intermediate step in assigning values to the former, raises certain issues. The issue of most importance in the present context is whether estimates of the solution parameter set **k** that is sought through the calibration process is compromised through adoption of the numerical convenience of estimating only a reduced set of parameters, and back-calculating **k** from the reduced set. Compromise may or may not be inevitable, depending upon the degree of parameter reduction that must be used, the nature of that reduction, and the characteristics of the system parameterization. If it is indeed inevitable, then it may be possible to reduce the detrimental effects of parameter reduction through understanding these effects and how they arise.

In this and the following section of this report, the nature of compromises incurred by the use of a reduced parameter set is explored. In the course of the discussion, two conditions are defined that, if fulfilled, result in no detrimental consequences incurred by the use of a reduced parameter set as an intermediary step in estimation of the detailed parameter set represented by **k**. The first of these defines the condition under which no structural noise is inflicted on model outputs corresponding to historical measurements of system state making up the calibration dataset by use of the reduced parameter set. The second of these defines the nature of the relation between the reduced and expanded parameter sets, which must exist for estimation of the reduced parameters to result in a maximum likelihood estimation of the expanded parameters.

Definition of Reduced Parameters

Let the vector **p** represent a set of reduced parameters that are estimated in place of **k**, estimation of **p** being preferable to estimation of **k** because of the (often vastly) reduced dimensionality of **p** with respect to that of **k**.

It is assumed that the inverse problem is still ill-posed, and thus that some form of mathematical regularization must be used for estimation of a parameter set **p**, which is deemed to "calibrate" the model. The advantages of regularized inversion over classical, overdetermined parameter estimation as a means of model calibration were discussed by Hunt and others (2007) and Moore and Doherty (2006), building on past work from Tikhonov (1963a, b), Parker (1977), Menke (1984), and Haber and others (1997). In particular, if undertaken properly and allowing adequate flexibility, it offers a better guarantee of achieving at least a good approximation to the maximum likelihood solution of the inverse problem than that offered by an over-simplified problem characterized by a greatly reduced parameter set made up of piecewise constant zones. Furthermore, representation of hydraulic complexity at a scale that more closely approximates that on which critical predictions may depend allows better quantification of the uncertainty associated with those predictions. See Tonkin and others (2007), Gallagher and Doherty (2007), and Tonkin and Doherty (2009) for more discussion of this point. In contrast, overdetermined calibration methodologies such as those described by Hill and Tiedeman (2007) require that a model-parameterization scheme serve the dual roles of (a) representation of hydraulic properties and (b) a regularization device. The need for a parameterization scheme to serve both of these roles may compromise its ability to serve either of them well. Furthermore, as Parker (1977) notes in the geophysical context:

> Sometimes, however, unknown structures are conceived in terms of small numbers of homogeneous layers for reasons of computational simplicity rather than on any convincing geophysical or geological grounds. Such simplification may lead to false confidence in the solution because the true amount of freedom has not been allowed in the parameters.

In the groundwater context, the lumping of parameter values into homogeneous zones constitutes an extreme and rigid imposition of prior information because once boundaries are delineated they cannot be changed by the parameter-estimation process. Although explicit methods to estimate both homogeneous zonal parameter values and their boundaries are in development (for example, Cardiff and Kitanidis, 2009), they are not commonly available and are computationally expensive.

The relation between parameters used by the model at the cell level (**j**), and the reduced parameter set (**p**) can be designated by the equation

$$\mathbf{j} = \mathbf{L}\mathbf{p}\,, \tag{14}$$

where **j** defines parameters on a grid scale (the same scale as **k**) and **p** defines the reduced set of parameters used for the purposes of parameter estimation. If **p** represents hydraulic properties assigned to pilot points, then the **L** matrix represents interpolation factors though which grid properties are computed by spatial interpolation from pilot-point properties. Alternatively, **p** may represent properties assigned to a large number of small zones of piecewise constancy. In this case, the **L** matrix is a "selection operator" through which each grid cell is assigned a property equal to that pertaining to the zone in which it lies.

Finally, $\underline{\mathbf{p}}$ represents a set of parameters estimated through the calibration process Equation 14 then becomes

$$\underline{\mathbf{k}} = \mathbf{L}\underline{\mathbf{p}}\,, \tag{15}$$

where $\underline{\mathbf{k}}$ represents calibrated model parameters at the cell scale.

Relation between Model and Reduced Parameters

A parameterization device used for calibration purposes is normally defined based on equation 14. This defines how model-grid properties are computed from the lumped parameter properties implied in the reduced parameter set **p**; in doing so, it defines the **L** matrix. It does not tell us, however, how lumped parameter properties are computed from grid properties. In fact, this latter relation (denoted herein as the matrix **N**) need not explicitly be known; however, there are desirable implicit attributes that this relation should possess. The remainder of this subsection describes these.

Notionally, we can compute a reduced parameter set **p** from the grid-level parameter field **k** using the following equation:

$$\mathbf{p} = \mathbf{N}\mathbf{k}\,. \tag{16}$$

If, for example, **p** represents the values assigned to zones of piecewise constancy, **N** may be an averaging matrix in which each row is composed of zero-valued elements, except for those elements that pertain to model cells that collectively comprise the zone pertaining to the respective element of **p**. Non-zero element values within a row of **N** may all have values of $1/n$, where n is the number of cells comprising the zone. Alternatively, a more complex averaging scheme could be adopted, whereby greater averaging weights are assigned to some cells (for example, those of greater area) than to others.

Though not necessarily known, **N** can be viewed as a generalized inverse of **L**. This is expressed as

$$\mathbf{N} = \mathbf{L}^{-} \tag{17}$$

and thus

$$\mathbf{L}\mathbf{N}\mathbf{L} = \mathbf{L}\,. \tag{18}$$

To clarify, consider that a cell-based parameter field **j** is computed from a set of reduced parameters **p** using equation 14 and that this field is then "re-reduced" to form another reduced parameter set. If that reduced parameter set is now expanded through application of equation 14, we should expect to obtain the same cell-based parameter field as we did on the first occasion of reduced parameter set expansion through application of equation 14.

Similarly, suppose that we start with a cell-based parameter field **k** and calculate a reduced parameter set using equation 16. If a new cell-based parameter field **j** is now computed from the reduced parameter set **p** using equation 14, and then a new set of parameters is computed from **j** using equation 16, we should expect to obtain the same reduced set that we obtained on the first application of **N**. That is, parameter reduction undertaken twice gives the same result as parameter reduction undertaken once, thus

$$\mathbf{N}\mathbf{L}\mathbf{N} = \mathbf{N}\,. \tag{19}$$

Given an **L**, there is no unique solution for **N**. A desirable choice for **N**, however, is

$$\mathbf{N} = (\mathbf{L}^T\mathbf{L})^{-1}\mathbf{L}^T \tag{20}$$

For pilot-point parameterization, equation 20 states that once pilot-point locations have been selected, the parameters **p** assigned to pilot points should be computed from a cell-based parameter field as that set of values that leads to minimized misfit in the least-squares sense between the starting field **k** and the parameter field **j** derived from pilot-point interpolation to the model grid or mesh. Where reduced parameters are zones, equation 20 stipulates that each zonal value (each element of **p**) is the average of respective **k** element values within the zone. Substitution readily verifies that **N** calculated through equation 20 satisfies equations 18 and 19.

Another choice for **N** is

$$\mathbf{N} = (\mathbf{L}^T\mathbf{Q}\mathbf{L})^{-1}\mathbf{L}^T\mathbf{Q}\,, \tag{21}$$

where **Q** is a matrix of full rank. If **Q** is a diagonal matrix, it can be considered as a weight matrix. Thus, for pilot points, the operation described by **N** through which lumping of **k** to form **p** is performed results in a set of pilot-point parameters for which the fit between the original and interpolated parameter fields is optimal in the weighted least-squares sense.

Where **p** describes zones of piecewise constancy, values assigned to zones are computed as a weighted average of cell values within each zone.

A weighting scheme can be such that, for each element of **p**, weights applied to the **k** field are zero for all but one cell of the model domain (that is, one element of **k**). Thus, values assigned to the elements of **p** can be considered as samples of the **k**-field. If such a scheme were used, it would follow that the sampled point coincided with the location of the respective pilot point or with the centroid of a zone if zone-based parameter reduction is used.

In practice, **N** is unknown; furthermore, it is model-specific. Therefore, although model-independent formulations such as equations 20 and 21 may satisfy certain of its requirements, they can only approximate the real **N**.

Note that if **N** were chosen rather than **L**, an **L** that satisfies equations 18 and 19 can be readily computed as

$$\mathbf{L} = \mathbf{N}^T(\mathbf{N}\mathbf{N}^T)^{-1} \tag{22a}$$

or

$$\mathbf{L} = \mathbf{Q}\mathbf{N}^T(\mathbf{N}\mathbf{Q}\mathbf{N}^T)^{-1}. \tag{22b}$$

The Reduced Model and One Condition for the Reduced Parameter Set

Equation 1 describes the relation between model parameters and observations comprising the calibration dataset; equation 3 describes this relation in the absence of measurement and structural noise. We will now derive the relation between model outputs and the reduced parameter set **p**.

Vector **o** describes a set of model outputs computed based on a reduced parameter set **p** so that

$$\mathbf{o} = \mathbf{X}\mathbf{p}, \tag{23}$$

where **X** is a matrix operator describing the action of the model on the parameter set **p** and **o** is the model-generated counterpart of **h** and contains the same number of elements. That is, the elements of **o** comprise a set of model outputs collocated with measurements of system state encapsulated in the **h** vector during the process of model calibration.

For every **p** there is a **j** described by equation 14. So the same set of model outputs **o** can be produced by the action of the cell-based model **Z** on a cell-based parameter field **j** as

$$\mathbf{o} = \mathbf{Z}\mathbf{j} = \mathbf{Z}\mathbf{L}\mathbf{p} \tag{24}$$

from which it is apparent that

$$\mathbf{X} = \mathbf{Z}\mathbf{L}. \tag{25}$$

When choosing a parameter-reduction scheme, undesirable artifacts of using the scheme under calibration conditions should be minimal or even zero. That is, it is best to use a scheme for which the differences between model outputs that correspond to members of the calibration dataset, computed based on a complex cell-based parameter set **k**, and those computed based on a simplified cell-based field **j** calculated from a reduced parameter set **p** using equation 14, are zero. In other words, the difference between **k** and **j** should lie in the null space of **Z**. Thus, the parameter reduction does not further degrade the solution beyond the effects of calibrating a model against a dataset of necessarily limited information content. In this case, adjusting values of the reduced parameter set **p** rather than the cell-based parameter set **k** during the calibration process, provides the same model output at the measurement of system state.

From equation 1,

$$\begin{aligned} \mathbf{h} &= \mathbf{Z}\mathbf{k} + \varepsilon \\ &= \mathbf{Z}\mathbf{k} - \mathbf{X}\mathbf{p} + \mathbf{X}\mathbf{p} + \varepsilon \\ &= \mathbf{X}\mathbf{p} + (\mathbf{Z}\mathbf{k} - \mathbf{X}\mathbf{p}) + \varepsilon \\ &= \mathbf{X}\mathbf{p} + \eta + \varepsilon \end{aligned} \tag{26}$$

from which it is apparent that the "structural noise" $\boldsymbol{\eta}$ incurred by using a reduced parameter set **p** is calculated as

$$\eta = (\mathbf{Z}\mathbf{k} - \mathbf{Z}\mathbf{p}). \tag{27}$$

Elimination of this noise (under calibration conditions) requires that

$$\begin{aligned} \mathbf{Z}\mathbf{k} &= \mathbf{X}\mathbf{p} \\ &= \mathbf{Z}\mathbf{L}\mathbf{p} \quad \text{(from equation 15)} \\ &= \mathbf{Z}\mathbf{L}\mathbf{N}\mathbf{k} \quad \text{(from equation 16)} \end{aligned} \tag{28}$$

from which we can derive the following equation as a desirable condition for the reduced parameterization scheme to satisfy

$$\mathbf{Z} = \mathbf{Z}\mathbf{L}\mathbf{N} = \mathbf{Z}\mathbf{L}\mathbf{L}^{-}. \tag{29}$$

This also can be written as

$$\mathbf{Z}(\mathbf{I} - \mathbf{L}\mathbf{N}) = \mathbf{Z}(\mathbf{I} - \mathbf{L}\mathbf{L}^{-}) = \mathbf{0} \tag{30}$$

denoting that ($\mathbf{I} - \mathbf{L}\mathbf{L}^{-}$) is in the null space of **Z**.

The conditions expressed by equations 29 and 30 can be approached by placing pilot points closer and closer together or by making zones of piecewise constancy smaller and smaller. In the limit, when a pilot point exists in every model cell of the model domain, or when every cell comprises its own zone, **L** becomes the identity matrix **I**, and equations 29 and 30 are exactly satisfied.

Equation 29 gives us the ability to calculate **N**, given an **L**. From equation 29

$$\mathbf{ZLN} = \mathbf{Z}$$
$$\mathbf{XN} = \mathbf{Z} \qquad \text{(from equation 25)}$$
$$\mathbf{X}^T\mathbf{XN} = \mathbf{X}^T\mathbf{Z}$$
$$(\mathbf{X}^T\mathbf{X})^{-1}\mathbf{X}^T\mathbf{XN} = (\mathbf{X}^T\mathbf{X})^{-1}\mathbf{X}^T\mathbf{Z}$$

and, thus

$$\mathbf{N} = (\mathbf{X}^T\mathbf{X})^{-1}\mathbf{X}^T\mathbf{Z}\,. \tag{31a}$$

N is still not unique, however, because it also could be calculated as

$$\mathbf{N} = (\mathbf{X}^T\mathbf{QX})^{-1}\mathbf{X}^T\mathbf{QZ}\,. \tag{31b}$$

Direct substitution (and use of equation 25) readily verifies that **N** calculated using either equation 31a or 31b satisfies both equations 18 and 19. In practice, **N** cannot be obtained through these equations because we do not know **Z**; computation of **Z** would require that derivatives of model outputs be calculated with respect to parameters assigned to every cell in the model domain. Although this is possible using adjoint-state methods such as those developed for MODFLOW-2005 by Clemo (written commun., 2007), it generally will not be feasible in contexts where reduced parameters are used, for the infeasibility of computing sensitivities at the grid-scale is the reason that reduced parameters are being used. Fortunately, there is little to be gained by knowing **N**. If an occasion arises where it is required, equation 20 or 21 can be used to compute approximations to **N**.

Two Key Conditions for Reduced Parameterization

Two key conditions follow, which constitute a successful reduced parameter set. The first is a condition regarding the selection of the pilot-point network, and the second involves the interpolation of the pilot-point values onto the computational model grid.

The first condition is established in equations 29 and 30. This condition states that the difference between the reduced parameter set (defined through pilot points and an interpolation scheme) and the full parameter set (defined as having a parameter value in every model cell) should be relegated to the null space of the relation between the full parameter set and the observations. The null space of this relation corresponds to parameter combinations about which values are not informed by observations comprising the calibration dataset. By relegating differences between the reduced and full parameter sets to the calibration null space, we can argue that there is a minimal loss of information in the calibration dataset incurred by using the reduced parameter set. The goal is to obtain the same estimate of parameter values as actually used by the model through adjustment of members of the reduced parameter set or the through adjustment of the full parameter set through the calibration process.

The second condition is discussed in equations 44 to 48, which shows that the interpolation function relating pilot-point values to model-cell parameter values ideally should be an orthogonal interpolator. An orthogonal interpolator is one for which interpolation basis functions, when multiplied by each other, integrate to zero over the model domain.

Taken together, these two conditions indicate that in an ideal situation, there should be many closely spaced pilot points and that grid values be derived from pilot-point values based on an orthogonal interpolation scheme. As will be shown, the second condition allows the first condition to be achieved using a smaller pilot-point density than would otherwise be the case. This is advantageous because the fewer pilot points that are used, the lower the computational burden of estimating the solution of the model calibration problem.

Pursuit of the Optimal Inverse

Model Parameters

As has already been discussed, the Moore-Penrose pseudoinverse has qualities that make it useful in solving the inverse problem in contexts where there is no measurement noise. Where there is measurement noise, however, the situation becomes more complex. A mathematical regularization scheme used to solve the inverse problem must then provide the means to restrict the goodness of model-to-measurement fit to a level that is commensurate with measurement (and structural) noise. This is possible when using Tikhonov regularization through calculation of an appropriate "regularization weight factor" (see Doherty, 2003, 2010 and Fienen and others, 2009, p. 837). If using truncated SVD as a regularization device, appropriate selection of the singular value that marks the boundary between the calibration solution and null spaces controls the balance of achieving a good fit with the need for regularization.

The intent of this report, however, is to explore the requirements of a reduced parameterization scheme. Insights into these requirements are best pursued in the context of no measurement noise where the demands on such a scheme are greatest. Conclusions drawn in this context then are extended to real-world contexts where measurement and structural noise are present and significant, thus reducing the demands placed on a reduced parameter scheme.

As stated above, where the innate variability of model parameters, represented by C(**k**), is homoscedastic, uncorrelated, and stationary (equation 7), the Moore-Penrose pseudoinverse provides the solution of maximum likelihood to the inverse problem. Unfortunately, however, hydraulic property spatial variability is unlikely to follow these conditions, for this would mean that properties in one cell of a model domain are statistically independent from those in neighboring cells. In most modeling contexts some spatial correlation is likely to exist. This must be accommodated in seeking an optimal solution to the inverse problem.

Singular value decomposition of a general C(**k**) leads to

$$\mathrm{C}(\mathbf{k}) = \mathbf{W}\mathbf{E}\mathbf{W}^{T}, \tag{32}$$

where the columns of **W** are orthogonal unit vectors that span parameter space, and **E** is a diagonal matrix containing the singular values of C(**k**), normally ranked in order of decreasing value. Because C(**k**) must be a positive definite matrix, none of these are zero, although some may be very small.

Let us now define a new parameter set **m** through transformation of the parameter set **k** as

$$\mathbf{m} = \mathbf{E}^{-1/2}\mathbf{W}^{T}\mathbf{k} \tag{33}$$

k is therefore calculated from **m** as

$$\mathbf{k} = \mathbf{W}\mathbf{E}^{1/2}\mathbf{m}\,. \tag{34}$$

From equation 33, the covariance matrix of **m** is

$$\mathrm{C}(\mathbf{m}) = \mathbf{I} \tag{35}$$

Therefore, **m** represents a suitable candidate for estimation using the Moore-Penrose pseudoinverse, and **k** then can be calculated from **m** using equation 34.

Orthogonal Basis Functions

If only a single parameter type within a single model layer is represented by the elements of **k**, the columns of **W** computed through equation 32 can be considered to form a set of orthogonal basis functions for **k** that span the domain of the model. In general, basis functions corresponding to high singular values depict broad-scale variation of the hydraulic property represented by **k**, while those corresponding to low singular values depict fine-scale variation of this property. The lowest singular values depict spatial variability at the model cell level. Figure 2*A* shows the first three and last three spatial eigencomponents of a covariance function computed from an exponential variogram over a rectangular model domain composed of 80 cells × 50 cells. The range (*a*) in the exponent of the variogram equation is equal to 10 cell widths. In the bottom panels, the apparent purple color is caused by elements of red (high) and blue (low) values alternating on a cell-by-cell basis. In other words, this figure represents extreme variability on a cell scale as opposed to the top panels, which show smoothly varying values at the scale of the entire image. Figure 2*B* shows the singular value spectrum of this covariance matrix, showing singular values in order of decreasing value. Taken together, these figures indicate that variability of broad-scale features is greater than variability of finer scale features.

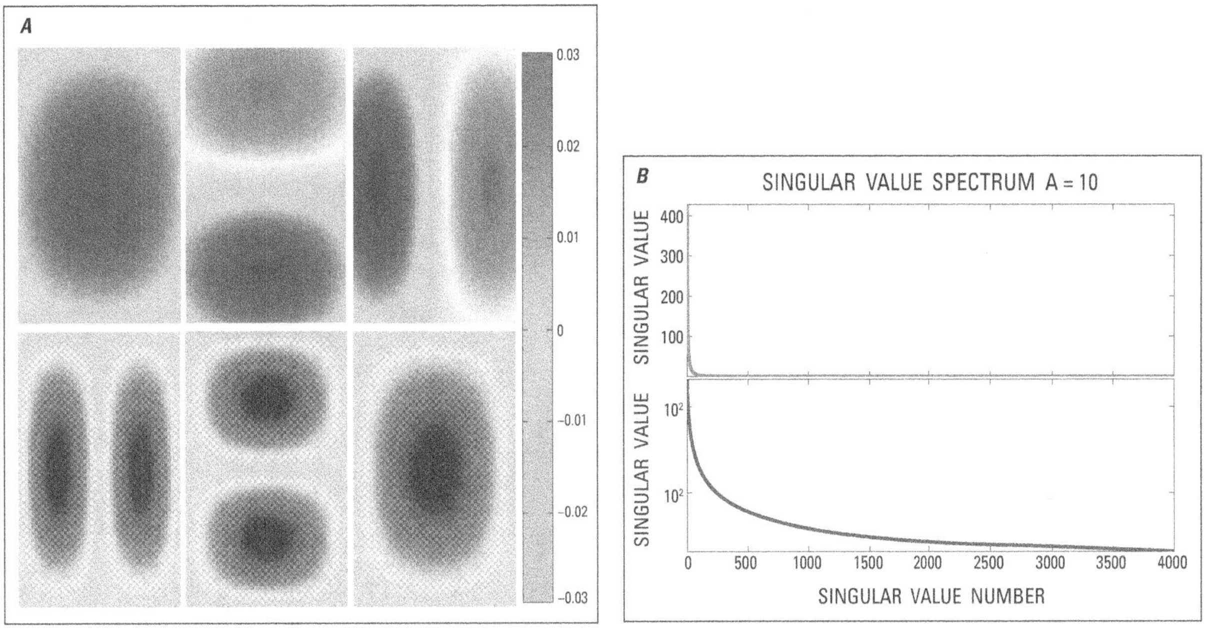

Figure 2. Graphical representation of singular vectors. Panel (*A*) shows the three first (top) and three last (bottom) singular vectors of the 80 row × 50 column exponential covariance matrix. Panel (*B*) shows the singular value spectrum of a covariance matrix on a linear scale (top) and logarithmic scale (bottom).

Because it is square, and because its columns are unit orthogonal vectors, $\mathbf{W}$ satisfies the following equations

$$\mathbf{W}^T\mathbf{W} = \mathbf{I}_m \qquad (36a)$$

$$\mathbf{W}\mathbf{W}^T = \mathbf{I}_m \, . \qquad (36b)$$

Here we add a subscript "m" to the identity matrix I to denote the fact that $\mathbf{I}$ is m-dimensional, where m is the number of elements of $\mathbf{k}$. As usual, the identity matrix is a diagonal matrix, with element values of 1 along the diagonal.

We partition $\mathbf{E}$ into two submatrices, the first containing the largest n singular values of $C(\mathbf{k})$, and the second containing the remaining m-n singular values

$$C(\mathbf{k}) = [\mathbf{W}_1 \quad \mathbf{W}_2]\begin{bmatrix} \mathbf{E}_1 & 0 \\ 0 & \mathbf{E}_1 \end{bmatrix}\begin{bmatrix} \mathbf{W}_1^T \\ \mathbf{W}_2^T \end{bmatrix} . \qquad (37)$$

That is,

$$C(\mathbf{k}) = \mathbf{W}_1\mathbf{E}_1\mathbf{W}_1^T + \mathbf{W}_2\mathbf{E}_2\mathbf{W}_2^T \, . \qquad (38)$$

The following equations hold:

$$\mathbf{W}_1^T\mathbf{W}_1 = \mathbf{I}_n \qquad (39a)$$

$$\mathbf{W}_2^T\mathbf{W}_2 = \mathbf{I}_{m\text{-}n} \qquad (39b)$$

$$\mathbf{W}_1\mathbf{W}_1^T + \mathbf{W}_2\mathbf{W}_2^T = \mathbf{I}_m \, . \qquad (40)$$

From equation 40, any vector $\mathbf{k}$ can be expressed as

$$\mathbf{k} = \mathbf{k}_1 + \mathbf{k}_2 = \mathbf{W}_1\mathbf{W}_1^T\mathbf{k} + \mathbf{W}_2\mathbf{W}_2^T\mathbf{k} \, . \qquad (41)$$

Equation 41 shows that any vector comprising a model parameter set $\mathbf{k}$ can be decomposed into two orthogonal vectors $\mathbf{k}_1$ and $\mathbf{k}_2$ by projecting k onto two orthogonal subspaces of parameter space, these being the subspaces spanned by the vectors comprising the columns of $\mathbf{W}_1$ and those comprising the columns of $\mathbf{W}_2$. $\mathbf{k}_1$ represents broad-scale hydraulic property variation (that is, variations that encompass lower spatial frequencies) because it is associated with the higher singular values of $C(\mathbf{k})$, while $\mathbf{k}_2$ represents localized hydraulic property detail (that is, variations of $\mathbf{k}$ associated with higher spatial frequencies). Equation 41 demonstrates that if $\mathbf{k}$ is decomposed in this manner, it is readily reconstituted by adding together the two orthogonal vectors resulting from this decomposition.

A Second Condition for the Reduced Parameter Set

So far, we have established one desirable condition for a reduced parameter set as the condition that differences between **j** and **k** lie in the null space of **Z**, encapsulated in equation 29. As stated above, a reduced parameter set will tend to satisfy this condition naturally as the dimensionality of **p** approaches that of **k**; however, we seek an ability to approach this condition even where the number of elements of **p** is much smaller than the number of elements of **k**, thereby maximizing the utility of the reduced parameter set. The smaller the reduced parameter set for which this condition is approximately fulfilled, the greater the numerical efficiency over the native model parameter set, as the numerical burden of estimating the reduced set of parameters diminishes with the size of this set. This leads to a second desirable condition for a reduced parameter set to meet.

Suppose that equation 29 is fulfilled (or almost fulfilled), and that there is little or no noise associated with the measurement dataset. Then

$$\mathbf{h} = \mathbf{Xp}\,. \tag{42}$$

Let us further suppose that the reduced parameter set **p** is defined in such a way that its covariance matrix of innate variability is proportional to the identity matrix $\mathbf{I}_n$. (Here we assume that it has n elements). Let us also assume that the native parameter set **k** from which it is reduced also is defined in such a way that its innate variability can be described by a covariance matrix that is proportional to $\mathbf{I}_m$ (whereby we assume that it has *m* elements). Thus, for example, the elements of **k** may be hydraulic properties pertaining to model cells, or more likely, they may be eigencomponents of the C(**k**) covariance matrix.

We are justified in using the Moore-Penrose pseudoinverse of **X** to solve for $\underline{\mathbf{p}}$, the calibrated reduced parameter set, because of the first of the above conditions. Thus, we can obtain $\underline{\mathbf{p}}$ as

$$\underline{\mathbf{p}} = \mathbf{X}^{+}\mathbf{h} \tag{43}$$

and then can obtain $\underline{\mathbf{k}}$ as

$$\begin{aligned}\underline{\mathbf{k}} &= \mathbf{LX}^{+}\mathbf{h} \\ &= \mathbf{L}(\mathbf{ZL})^{+}\mathbf{h}\end{aligned} \tag{44}$$

where the second relation follows from equation 25. For $\underline{\mathbf{k}}$ as computed using equation 44 to be optimal, the following relation must hold:

$$\mathbf{Z}^{+} = \mathbf{L}(\mathbf{ZL})^{+}\,. \tag{45}$$

Direct substitution of equation 45 into equations 6a-d readily establishes that equation 45 holds, provided that equation 29 holds, and provided that one extra condition is satisfied;

$$\mathbf{L}^{-} = \alpha\mathbf{L}^{T}\,, \tag{46}$$

where α is an arbitrary scalar. Now, from

$$\mathbf{LL}^{-}\mathbf{L} = \mathbf{L} \tag{47}$$

we obtain

$$\begin{aligned}&\mathbf{L}\alpha\mathbf{L}^{T}\mathbf{L} = \mathbf{L} \qquad \text{(from equation 46)}\\ &\alpha\mathbf{L}(\mathbf{L}^{T}\mathbf{L}) = \mathbf{L}\\ &\alpha\mathbf{L}(\mathbf{L}^{T}\mathbf{L})(\mathbf{L}^{T}\mathbf{L})^{-1} = \mathbf{L}(\mathbf{L}^{T}\mathbf{L})^{-1}\\ &\mathbf{L} = \mathbf{L}(\mathbf{L}^{T}\mathbf{L})^{-1}/\alpha\\ &\mathbf{L}^{T} = (\mathbf{L}^{T}\mathbf{L})^{-1}\mathbf{L}^{T}/\alpha\\ &\mathbf{L}^{T}\mathbf{L} = \mathbf{I}/\alpha\end{aligned} \tag{48}$$

Equation 48 shows that the interpolation or basis functions through which cell-based parameters are computed from reduced parameters must be orthogonal. Note also that substitution of equation 48 into the right side of equation 20 immediately leads to equation 46, recalling that **N** in equation 20 is $\mathbf{L}^{-}$.

This has several repercussions. Where the reduced parameter set is composed of zones of piecewise constancy (presumably enough of these for equation 29 to hold), then **L** is "naturally" orthogonal. It also is naturally orthogonal if a nearest-neighbor interpolation scheme is implemented about pilot points (which amounts to the same thing). It is not orthogonal, however, if interpolation is undertaken using, for example, triangle basis functions or Kriging.

If parameterization is based on eigencomponents **m** of C(**k**) defined by equation 33, and if parameter reduction is effected through selection of only the first *n* (out of *m*) of these, **L** is simply a diagonal "selection matrix," an example of which is shown below, where *m* is 6 and *n* is 3:

$$\mathbf{L} = \begin{bmatrix} 1 & 0 & 0 & 0 & 0 & 0 \\ 0 & 1 & 0 & 0 & 0 & 0 \\ 0 & 0 & 1 & 0 & 0 & 0 \\ 0 & 0 & 0 & 0 & 0 & 0 \\ 0 & 0 & 0 & 0 & 0 & 0 \end{bmatrix}. \tag{49}$$

This matrix satisfies equation 48.

Application to Pilot Points

Where pilot points are used as a basis for reduced model parameterization, **L** could take many forms. As stated above, if a nearest-neighbor interpolation scheme is used, this is equivalent to the use of polygonal zones of piecewise constancy. Each row of the **L** matrix is then composed of zeroes, except for a single element of value 1, which assigns to a model cell a hydraulic property value equal to that pertaining to the closest pilot point. More complex interpolation schemes, such as Kriging, have far fewer (if any) zero-valued elements.

In spite of the diversity of interpolation schemes that could be used, there are some things they must have in common. Ideally, a spatial interpolation scheme should be such that it honors the value assigned to each pilot point, no matter the value. This requires that the value of the interpolation function pertaining to every pilot point be 1.0 at the location of that point, and 0.0 at the location of other pilot points (assuming that pilot points are placed at cell centers and that hydraulic property values are assigned to these same locations).

For some schemes, element values along any row of the L matrix sum to 1.0. Thus, if all pilot points are assigned the same value, all model cells will be assigned that same value. In many circumstances this is a desirable property; however, this may not always be the case. For example, it may be desired that interpolated values approach some preferred value if they are too far from the nearest pilot point; simple Kriging has this property.

Two further desirable properties arise from the condition expressed by equation 29:

1. Pilot points should be close together where data density is high; and
2. The interpolation function encapsulated in the columns of **L** should avoid "sharp edges," unless these coincide with known geologic contacts or other real discontinuities.

Lack of adherence to either of the above properties is likely to generate parameterization-induced structural noise, both of these leading to an erosion of the extent to which equation 29 is respected by a reduced parameterization scheme.

From equation 48, arises the added desirability of an orthogonal interpolation scheme.

Tikhonov Regularization

Tikhonov Regularization and the Generalized Inverse

As discussed previously, where parameters **k** are characterized by a covariance matrix C(**k**), optimality of the inverse problem solution is achieved in the absence of measurement noise by first estimating parameters **m** using the Moore-Penrose pseudoinverse, and then computing **k** from that **m** using equation 34.

With the role of SVD in obtaining the Moore-Penrose pseudoinverse explained previously, equation 13 can be used to find the Moore-Penrose pseudoinverse, then to estimate **m**. From equation 34, **A** in equation 13 becomes **ZL**, where **L** is given by

$$\mathbf{L} = \mathbf{W}\mathbf{E}^{1/2}. \tag{50}$$

Direct substitution into equation 13 then leads to estimation of **m** through

$$\mathbf{m} = \lim_{\delta \to 0}[\mathbf{E}^{1/2}\mathbf{W}^T\mathbf{Z}^T\mathbf{Z}\mathbf{W}\mathbf{E}^{1/2} + \delta^2\mathbf{I}]^{-1}\mathbf{E}^{1/2}\mathbf{W}^T\mathbf{Z}^T\mathbf{h}. \tag{51}$$

Use of equation 34 again, and a little manipulation, then leads to

$$\mathbf{k} = \lim_{\delta \to 0}[\mathbf{Z}^T\mathbf{Z} + \delta^2\mathrm{C}^{-1}(\mathbf{k})]^{-1}\mathbf{Z}^T\mathbf{h}. \tag{52}$$

Extending the discussion provided by De Groot-Hedlin and Constable (1990) and Doherty (2003), equation 52 could be obtained by solution of a constrained minimization problem:

Minimize $\Phi_\mathrm{r} = \mathbf{k}^T\mathrm{C}^{-1}(\mathbf{k})\mathbf{k}$ subject to the constraint that:

$$\begin{aligned}&\Phi_\mathrm{m} = (\mathbf{h} - \mathbf{Zk})^T(\mathbf{h} - \mathbf{Zk}) = \Phi_m^l \\ &\text{as } \Phi_m^l \to 0\end{aligned} \tag{53}$$

This formulation of the calibration process seeks the (unique) solution to the inverse problem for which parameters deviate minimally (based on a C(**k**) norm) from a pre-calibration maximum likelihood condition of $\Phi_\mathrm{r} = 0$. In this formulation, which is used in PEST, the constraint Φ_m^l (referred to in PEST as PHIMLIM) controls the strength of regularization. This is closely related to Occam's inversion (Constable and others, 1987). Guidelines for adjusting Φ_m^l using basic statistics are presented in Doherty (2003) and Fienen and others (2009). An alternative, such as cross validation (see Kitanidis, 1997 or Aster and others, 2005), could be implemented as well.

Alternatively, equation 52 can be viewed as a traditional parameter-estimation problem:

Find **k** such that:

$$\begin{aligned}&\mathbf{h} = \mathbf{Zk} + \boldsymbol{\varepsilon} && (\text{where } \mathrm{C}(\varepsilon) = \delta^2\mathbf{I}) \\ &\mathbf{k} = \mathbf{0} + \boldsymbol{\tau} && (\text{where } \mathrm{C}(\tau) = \mathrm{C}(\mathbf{k})) \\ &\text{as } \delta^2 \to 0\end{aligned} \tag{54}$$

Accommodation of Measurement Noise

We have seen that estimation of **m** (equal to $\mathbf{E}^{-1/2}\mathbf{W}^T\mathbf{k}$) using SVD, or **k** using Tikhonov regularization, leads to the same solution of the inverse problem where noise is zero. Where noise is not zero, a perfect fit between model outputs and field data cannot be expected and should not be sought; however, Tikhonov and subspace regularization (that is, SVD) diverge in the means that they employ to obtain a model-to-measurement misfit, which is commensurate with the level of measurement noise. In particular:

1. Where SVD is used as a regularization device, the truncation level is shifted to a singular value of greater magnitude.

2. Where Tikhonov regularization is used, the target measurement objective function Φ_m^l is raised.

Both methods have limitations, especially when applied in real-world settings, where **C**(**k**) and **C**(ε) are known only with some degree of uncertainty. In contexts where **C**(**k**) exhibits highly nonstationary behavior, use of Tikhonov regularization applied as equation 53 leads to a certain amount of "double accounting" of parameter constraints, which can lead to numerical problems in its application. In particular, for a non-zero δ^2, use of equation 54 implies that there are two (sometimes contradicting) sources of information on solution space components of **k**. These have their sources in (a) the measurement dataset and (b) the regularization term through its suggestion that elements of **k** are all zero valued. In many contexts this problem can be at least partially rectified (with a consequential improvement in the numerical behavior of Tikhonov regularization) through reformulation of equation 54 in the presence of measurement noise as:

Find **k** such that

$$
\begin{aligned}
\mathbf{h} &= \mathbf{Zk} + \varepsilon \\
&= \mathbf{Z}(\mathbf{V}_1\mathbf{V}_1^T + \mathbf{V}_2\mathbf{V}_2^T)\mathbf{k} + \varepsilon \\
&= \mathbf{Z}\mathbf{V}_1\mathbf{V}_1^T\mathbf{k} + \xi \qquad (\text{where } \xi = \mathbf{V}_2\mathbf{V}_2^T\mathbf{k} \text{ and } C(\xi) \approx \sigma_r^2\mathbf{I} \\
\mathbf{0} &= \mathbf{V}_2\mathbf{V}_2^T\mathbf{k} + \tau \qquad (\text{where } C(\tau) = \mathbf{V}_2\mathbf{V}_2^T C(\mathbf{k})\mathbf{V}_2\mathbf{V}_2^T
\end{aligned}
$$

where, through SVD

$$\mathbf{Z} = \mathbf{USV}^T \tag{55}$$

and **V** is partitioned into $\mathbf{V}_1$ and $\mathbf{V}_2$ submatrices at the SVD truncation point that is chosen to separate calibration solution and null spaces. With this subspace enhancement formulation, Tikhonov regularization is applied to null space components of **k** while solution space components of **k** are estimated from the calibration dataset; the operation of one does not thereby interfere with that of the other.

Strictly speaking, C(ξ) should account for structural noise incurred through truncation, if truncation occurs prior to singular values becoming absolutely zero; however, this is rarely done owing to the numerical work involved in calculating its covariance matrix (using, for example, the paired stochastic analysis of Cooley, 2004). Furthermore, the need for its inclusion is somewhat mitigated by the fact that far less regularization-based structural noise needs to be included in the above formation than in the overdetermined formulation discussed by Cooley (2004), where model parameterization must serve the dual roles of regularization and representation of hydraulic properties.

The formulation in equation 55 is further examined (and refined) in the "Theory" section of this report. Subspace enhancement of Tikhonov regularization (which uses both this and other similar formulations) is available through PEST.

Spatial Covariance

Cell-by-Cell Independence

Suppose that hydraulic properties within a model domain possess a covariance matrix that is proportional to the identity matrix;

$$C(\mathbf{k}) = \sigma_k^2\mathbf{I}\,. \tag{56}$$

Through use of equation 32, a set of orthogonal basis functions that complement this C(**k**) matrix can be found. Any distribution of hydraulic properties **k** then can be expressed in terms of this set of basis functions; however, because decomposition of equation 56 leads to a singular value matrix **E**, which is in fact the identity matrix **I**, we have unlimited freedom in choosing our basis functions. All that is required is that they are orthogonal, that they span parameter space, and that each has a magnitude of unity; they will therefore satisfy equations 36a and 36b. For example, we could choose basis functions that arise from application of SVD to a covariance matrix arising from any useful variogram. Alternatively, we could choose "blocky" basis functions such as are depicted in one dimension in figure 2.

For the set of basis functions to span the entirety of parameter space, the trend of increasing frequency apparent in figure 3 would need to extend to the point where spatial variability occurs at the cell level; the corresponding basis function simply would oscillate between its upper and lower bounds, with the transition between the two occurring at cell boundaries.

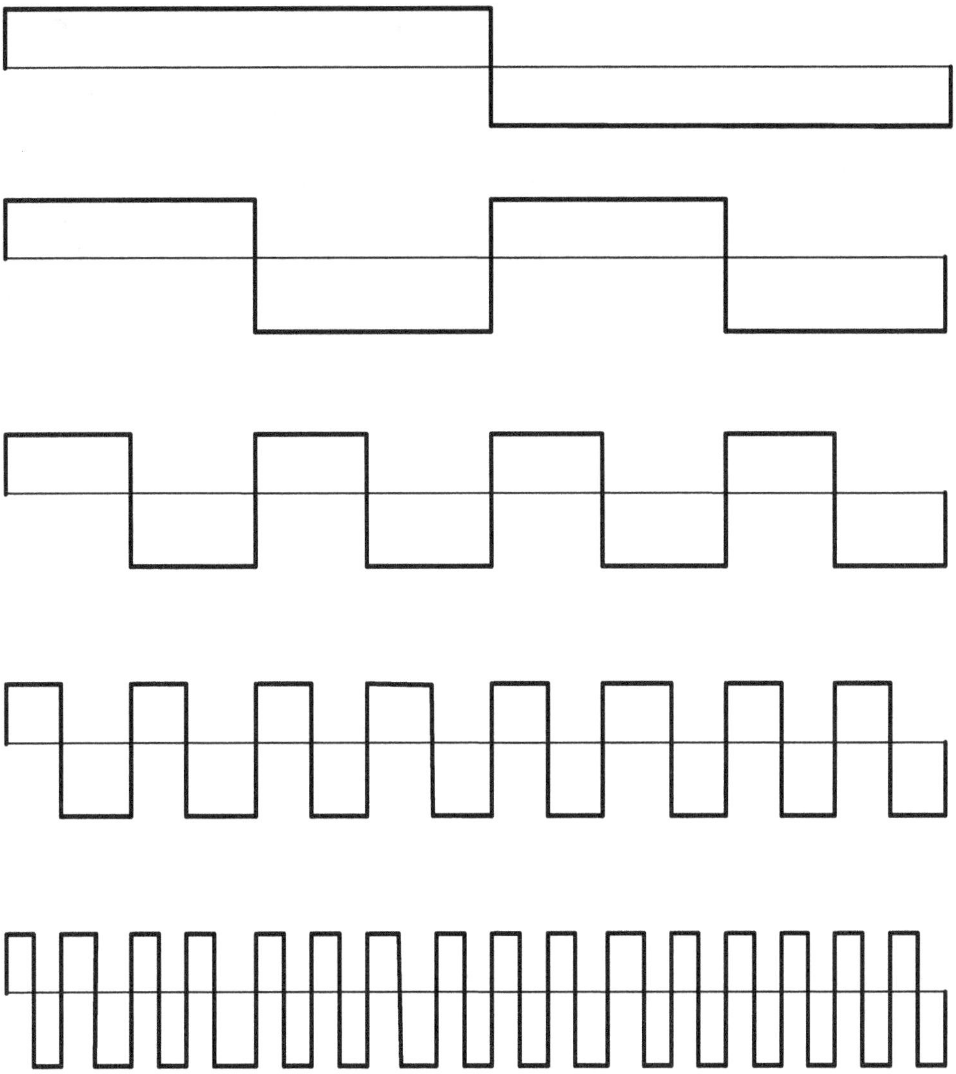

Figure 3. A set of orthogonal basis functions in one dimension.

Spectra

Suppose now that pilot points are distributed evenly throughout a model domain. Let **L** be chosen to implement nearest-neighbor interpolation. Equation 48 then dictates that **N** be an averaging matrix. The value assigned to each pilot point can thus be considered to represent the average value of the native hydraulic property field (the **k** field) over an interval equal to the pilot-point separation distance, with the respective point at the center of each such interval. Furthermore, α of equation 48 is equal to 1.

The upper part of figure 4 shows a native hydraulic property field, where variability occurs randomly and independently on a cell-by-cell basis. Pilot-point locations are shown in the middle part of the figure; the values assigned to these points through interval averaging are represented by their elevations. Note, that in this figure, it is assumed that the scale of model cells is not very fine, the resulting "granularity" in the **k** field being readily apparent. The final segment of figure 4 shows the "**j** field," this being the field reconstructed from pilot points based on equation 14.

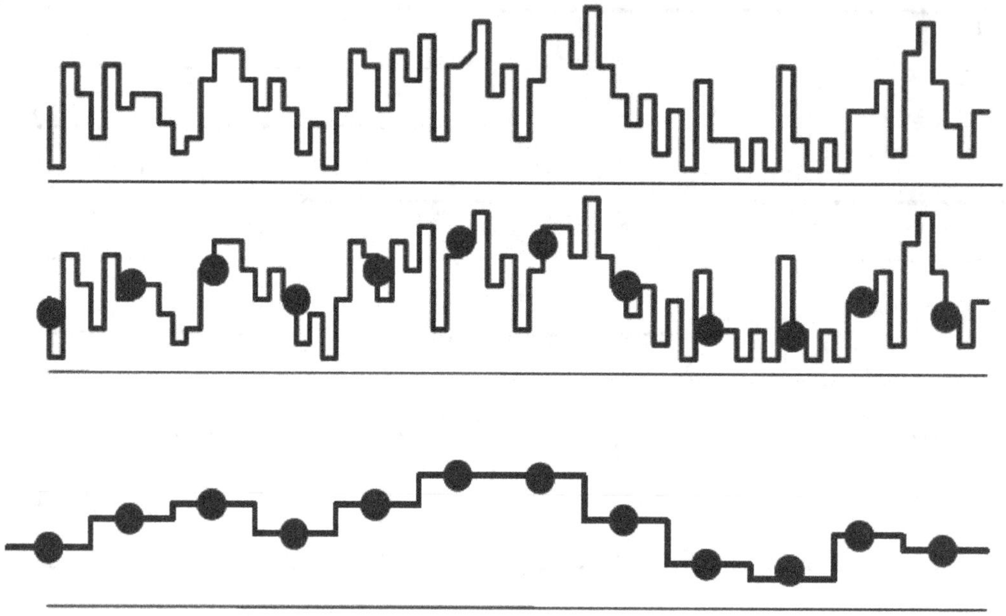

Figure 4. A sampled and reconstituted spatially varying hydraulic-property field.

From a mathematical perspective, from equations 14, 16, and 17

$$\mathbf{j} = \mathbf{LNk} = \mathbf{LL}^{-}\mathbf{k}\,. \qquad (57)$$

The spatial covariance matrix of **j** is thus

$$\begin{aligned} C(\mathbf{j}) &= \mathbf{LL}^{-}C(\mathbf{k})\mathbf{L}^{-T}\mathbf{L}^{T} \\ &= \sigma_k^2\mathbf{LL}^{-}\mathbf{L}^{-T}\mathbf{L}^{T} \quad \text{(from equation 56)} \\ &= \sigma_k^2\mathbf{LL}^{-}\mathbf{LL}^{T} \quad \text{(from equation 46 with } \alpha\text{=1)} \\ &= \sigma_k^2\mathbf{LL}^{T} \quad \text{(from equation 4)} \end{aligned} \qquad (58)$$

From equations 58 and 38 the singular vectors of C(**j**) whose singular values are non-zero are formed by the (orthogonal) columns of **L**. Thus, the interpolation function (this being equivalent to zones of piecewise constancy in the present case) forms a set of orthogonal basis functions. These orthogonal basis functions do not, however, have the capacity to carry as much detail as is required to represent an arbitrary **k** field. To learn something of the loss of detail incurred by sampling and then reconstitution, we can rewrite C(**j**) (with the help of equation 36b) as

$$C(\mathbf{j}) = \sigma_k^2\mathbf{LL}^{-}\mathbf{WIW}^{T}\mathbf{L}^{-T}\mathbf{L}^{T}, \qquad (59)$$

where the columns of **W** are composed of the basis functions of figure 3 (and **I** is the identity matrix as usual). If the pilot-point emplacement frequency is a power of 2 multiple of the primary basis function frequency (corresponding to the top graph of figure 3), equation 59 can be rewritten without changing its value by replacing **I** with a matrix that has lost some of its 1's and therefore acts as a "selection" matrix, selecting only those columns of **W** that collectively comprise a submatrix $\mathbf{W}_1$ for which

$$\mathbf{LL}^{-}\mathbf{W}_1 = \mathbf{W}_1 \qquad (60a)$$

therefore, for which (from equation 48 with $\alpha = 1$)

$$\mathbf{LL}^{T}\mathbf{W}_1 = \mathbf{W}_1\,. \qquad (60b)$$

The columns of $\mathbf{W}_1$ are those basis functions that are unaffected by sampling and reconstitution. In the schematic of figure 4, these will be the top two basis functions, but not the bottom one. That is, they are the basis functions that describe **k** variations, which take place at a broader scale than that of the sampling interval. Substituting equation 60a into 59 produces

$$C(\mathbf{j}) = \sigma_k^2\mathbf{W}_1\mathbf{W}_1^{T}\,. \qquad (61)$$

By including as many basis functions in $\mathbf{W}_1$ as the emplacement frequency allows, it then follows that

$$\mathbf{LL}^{T}\mathbf{W}_2 = \mathbf{0}\,. \qquad (62)$$

Sampling and reconstitution removes high spatial frequencies, because the summation implied in $\mathbf{L}^T$ averages them to zero over each averaging interval. (They are equally positive and negative over each such interval).
From this analysis, we conclude that:

1. Two (in fact many) families of basis functions can be used to represent the reconstituted parameter field. These include those composed of the interpolation functions, as well as basis functions inherited from the original spatial covariance matrix of **k**.

2. In the case of inherited basis functions, only a subset of basis functions is inherited. For the regular sampling interval used in the present example, these represent the basis functions with a spatial frequency that is less than half that of pilot-point emplacement.

3. Spatial frequencies within the original **k** field that are greater than half the pilot-point emplacement interval are lost or "filtered out" through representation of that field by pilot points.

This is exactly analogous to the Nyquist frequency in sampling theory (see Roberts, 2004, p. 503).

The fact that high spatial frequencies are lost where a parameter field is represented using pilot points may not matter for the particular problem objective. For example, fine-scale parameter heterogeneity is more important for contaminant-transport problems than for water-balance problems. In fact, we attempt to ensure that it does not matter by selecting a sufficiently dense pilot-point emplacement interval and appropriate interpolation method for this to be the case. From equations 29 and 46

$$\mathbf{Z} = \mathbf{ZLL}^{-} = \mathbf{ZLL}^{T} . \tag{63}$$

Post-multiplying equation 63 by $\mathbf{W}_2$ and invoking equation 62 we have

$$\mathbf{ZW}_2 = \mathbf{0} . \tag{64}$$

Thus, the components of the parameter field that are lost through representation of that field using pilot points lay in the null space of the model. Therefore, they were never informed or constrained by the calibration process.

Finally, using equations 56 and 61 we can draw singular value spectra of the **k** and **j** parameter fields (fig. 5), which illustrates the low-pass filtering effect of pilot-point usage. The reader is reminded, however, that this desirable low-pass filtering effect relies on the following aspects of the design of our pilot-point scheme:

1. The interpolation matrix **L** implements nearest-neighbor interpolation; $\mathbf{L}^T$ is thus an averaging function.

2. The spacing of pilot points must be such that "breaks" in the $\mathbf{L}^T$ averaging function occur at the same locations as those of the eigenfunctions of figure 3.

The above analysis does not depend on cell-by-cell statistical independence of the **k** parameter field, as was assumed in the above discussion. If C(**k**) were in fact represented by equation 32 with a singular value spectrum in which variance (singular value magnitude) decreases with increasing singular value number (and therefore with increasing spatial frequency), the situation would be as shown in figure 6. Spectra such as represented in the upper part of figure 6, where features embodied in hydraulic property heterogeneity tend to extend over a multiplicity of cells, are much more in accordance with real-world hydraulic property variability than that depicted in the upper part of figure 5 where statistical independence of cell properties is depicted.

Geological and hydrogeological phenomena, though unknown on a point-by-point basis, are known to show some degree of spatial continuity. This continuity is expressed geostatistically through use of a variogram or (equivalently) through use of a covariance matrix of spatial variability as is done here. In other disciplines, concepts such as "spatial frequency power spectra" are used to represent the same phenomena. The two concepts are related and others (Philip and Watson, 1986) suggest that use of geostatistics instead of spatial frequency spectra as a basis for spatial analysis is of limited use even though tools based on the latter concept have been used in other disciplines to great effect. Nevertheless, characterization of spatial variability based on covariance matrices is useful when consideration is turned to uncertainty analysis; thus, it is retained for this report.

Use of a Variogram-Based Spatial Covariance Matrix

C(**k**) represents the covariance matrix of spatial variability at a particular study site. This often is based on a variogram, even if detailed geostatistical studies have not been carried out at that site. Use of a variogram, together with the simultaneous assumption of stationarity, allows easy construction of a C(**k**) matrix. It also allows easy calculation of geostatistical products such as Kriging factors and random parameter fields. In hydrogeological studies, choice of a variogram type normally is more of a matter of convenience, though the exponential variogram is frequently chosen.

Implicit in the choice of a particular covariance matrix of spatial variability is the choice of a set of orthogonal basis functions spanning the model domain as in equation 32, repeated here

$$C(\mathbf{k}) = \mathbf{WEW}^{T} . \tag{65}$$

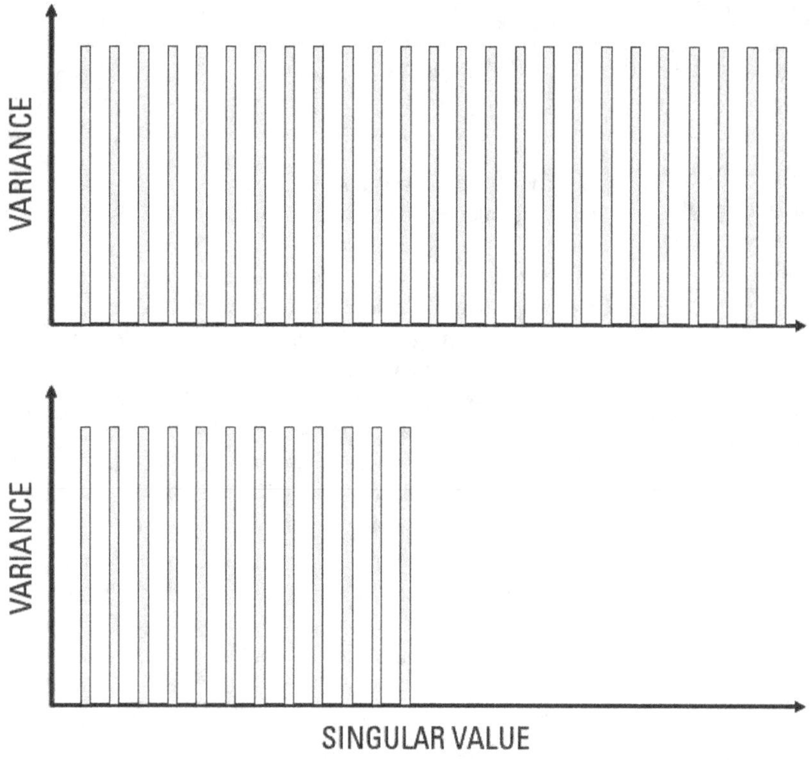

Figure 5. Spectrum of a cell-by-cell parameter field (above) and of the equivalent pilot-point sampled parameter field (below). Statistical independence of cell properties is represented in the former case.

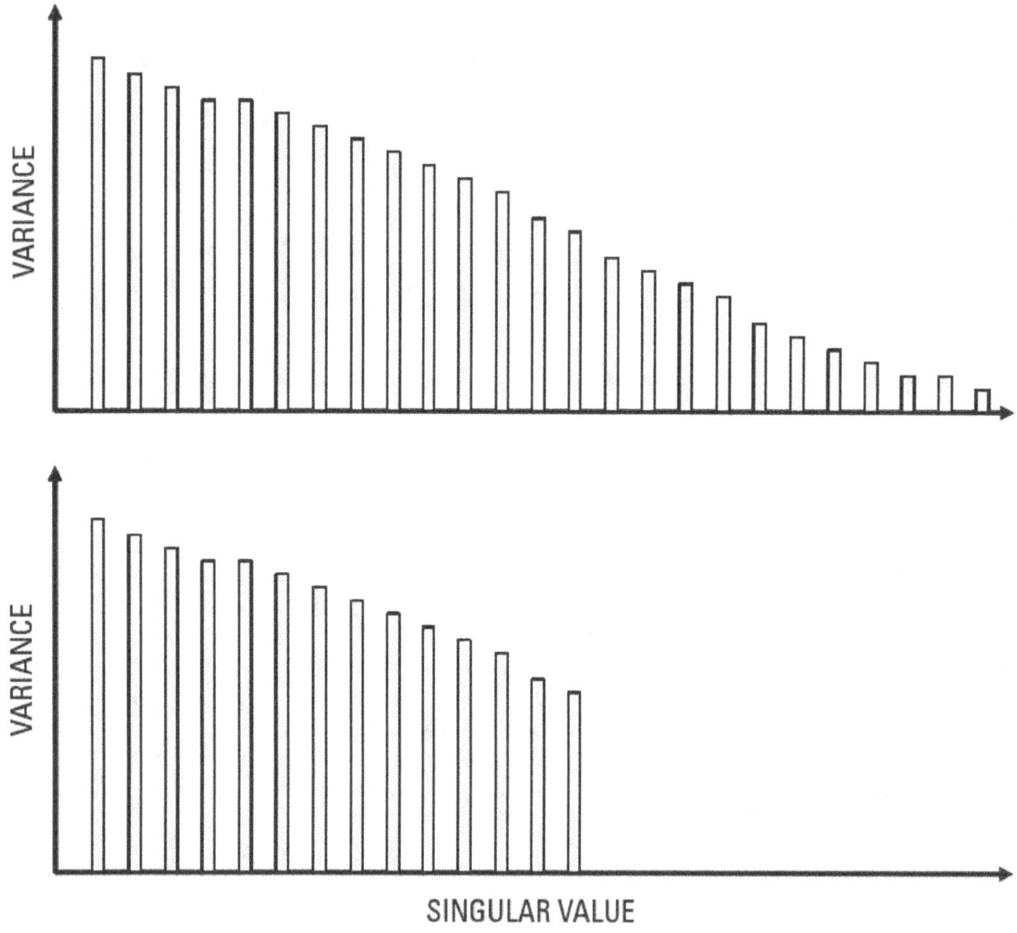

Figure 6. Spectrum of a cell-by-cell parameter field (above) and of the equivalent pilot-point sampled parameter field (below). Spatial correlation of cell properties is characterized in both cases.

As discussed above, the basis functions are the columns of **W**. Suppose now that a set of pilot points is used as a means of parameter reduction (implemented for the purpose of model calibration), together with a set of interpolation coefficients **L**. Suppose also that in emplacing pilot points and in interpolating between them, the two conditions discussed in previous sections are honored:

$$\mathbf{ZLL}^{-} = \mathbf{Z} \quad (66)$$

$$\mathbf{L}^{-} = \alpha\mathbf{L}^{T} . \quad (67a)$$

Thus,

$$\mathbf{L}^{T}\mathbf{L} = \mathbf{I}/\alpha . \quad (67b)$$

Choice of **L** leads immediately to $\mathbf{L}^{-}$ (and therefore **N** of equation 16), because of equation 67a. Conceptually at least, we know what is being estimated through the inversion process. In addition, conceptually at least, this formulation may be used in a structural noise analysis (Cooley, 2004) to minimize the effect of parameter reduction on estimation error.

In the analysis of the previous section, basis functions and interpolation functions were such that the covariance matrix of the reconstructed parameter field (the **j** field) contains many of the characteristics of the original parameter field (the **k** field). This allows easy visualization of the effects of using a reduced parameter set; however, where basis functions are chosen based on a selected covariance matrix, and where pilot points are not necessarily regularly spaced, the situation unfortunately is not as clear.

As above, let **p** represent a reduced set of parameters (in this case pilot points) that are used as a basis for calibration-based parameterization of a model. Then

$$\mathbf{p} = \mathbf{Nk} = \mathbf{L}^{-}\mathbf{k} = \alpha\mathbf{L}^{T}\mathbf{k} \quad (68)$$

so that

$$\mathrm{C}(\mathbf{p}) = \alpha^{2}\mathbf{L}^{T}\mathrm{C}(\mathbf{k})\mathbf{L} = \alpha^{2}\mathbf{L}^{T}\mathbf{WEW}^{T}\mathbf{L} . \quad (69)$$

From equation 69, it is apparent that the covariance matrix (or variogram) pertaining to a set of pilot points is not the same as that attributed to the **k** parameter field. Pilot-point parameters do not have the same statistical properties as cell-based parameters, for account must be taken of the averaging process encapsulated in the $\mathbf{L}^{-}$ matrix through which pilot-point parameters are related to cell-based parameters.

The covariance matrix of the reconstituted parameter field **j** is

$$\mathrm{C}(\mathbf{j}) = \alpha^{2}\mathbf{LL}^{T}\mathrm{C}(\mathbf{k})\mathbf{LL}^{T} = \alpha^{2}\mathbf{LL}^{T}\mathbf{WEW}^{T}\mathbf{LL}^{T} . \quad (70)$$

The situation shown in figure 6 can occur exactly as depicted only if **L** is chosen such that equations 60 and 62 are followed. If such an **L** can be found, it will form a "natural" interpolation method to accompany the pilot points and chosen covariance matrix. Unfortunately, this is not an easy matter. Moreover, selection of which singular vectors to include in $\mathbf{W}_1$ and $\mathbf{W}_2$ would become especially problematic with irregular pilot-point emplacement. Therefore, selection of a useful L can be approximate only. This is a matter that requires research, and is discussed in the last section of this report. For now, however, we can state that the desirable properties of **L** are that

$$\mathbf{L}^{T}\mathbf{W}_2 = 0 \quad (71)$$

where $\mathbf{W}_2$ is as full as possible, yet satisfies

$$\mathbf{ZW}_2 = 0 . \quad (72)$$

Equation 71 is derived by pre-multiplying both sides of equation 62 by $(\mathbf{L}^{T}\mathbf{L})^{-1}\mathbf{L}^{T}$.

Singular Vectors and Interpolation

p is a vector of reduced parameters (for example, pilot-point parameters), and cell-based parameters are obtained from them using equation 14, which can be rewritten as

$$\mathbf{j} = \mathbf{Lp} . \quad (73)$$

Suppose that **p** is characterized by a covariance matrix C(**p**) and that **e** is a singular vector of this matrix. Thus,

$$\mathrm{C}(\mathbf{p})\mathbf{e} = \lambda\mathbf{e} . \quad (74)$$

The covariance matrix of **j** is given by

$$\mathrm{C}(\mathbf{j}) = \mathbf{L}\mathrm{C}(\mathbf{p})\mathbf{L}^{T} . \quad (75)$$

Since the elements of **j** outnumber those of **p**, C(**j**) is rank-deficient (and therefore singular), possessing only the same number of non-zero singular values as C(**p**) from which it is derived. From equation 75,

$$\begin{aligned} \mathrm{C}(\mathbf{j})\mathbf{Le} &= \mathbf{L}\mathrm{C}(\mathbf{p})\mathbf{L}^{T}\mathbf{Le} \\ &= \mathbf{L}\mathrm{C}(\mathbf{p})\mathbf{e}/\alpha \qquad \text{if equation 67b holds} \\ &= \lambda\mathbf{Le}/\alpha \qquad \text{(from equation 74)} \quad . \quad (76) \end{aligned}$$

Thus, if **L** is chosen such that equation 67b is followed, the singular vectors of C(**j**) whose singular values are non-zero are computed from those of C(**p**) by spatial interpolation of the singular vectors of this latter matrix. (In other words, they will look the same if plotted spatially as in figure 2). Furthermore, relativity between singular values is maintained; in fact, singular values will be the same between the two matrices if α is unity.

Suppose now that C(**p**) is subjected to singular value decomposition such that

$$C(\mathbf{p}) = \mathbf{UFU}^T . \tag{77}$$

Suppose also that, in ways discussed previously, we obtain a minimum norm solution for eigencomponent parameters **n** related to parameters **p** using the formula

$$\mathbf{n} = \mathbf{F}^{-1/2}\mathbf{U}^T\mathbf{p} . \tag{78}$$

Because the elements of **n** are statistically independent and have identical variances (similar to the elements of **m** in the previous discussion, see equation 35), the minimum norm solution for **n** also is the maximum likelihood solution for **n**. The maximum likelihood solution for **p** then can be computed from **n**. Because **j** has identical eigencomponents to those of **p**, the maximum likelihood solution for **j** also can be calculated from that of **n**. In other words, interpolation using a matrix **L**, chosen to follow equation 67b, has neither introduced spurious information to the interpolated parameter set nor violated the maximum likelihood nature of the solution to the inverse problem found for **p**.

This relation is useful, in that calibration needs only to focus on achieving maximum likelihood for the reduced parameter set **p**; the maximum likelihood for cell-based parameters **j** will follow. A problem with this approach, however, is that achievement of a maximum likelihood solution of the inverse problem for the reduced parameter set **p** does not necessarily guarantee that a maximum likelihood solution has been found for the true parameter set **k** of which **p** is a reduced representation. This will occur only if equations 60, 62, and 64 are followed which as stated above, may not be possible, and often can be approximated only.

Kriging as an Interpolator

Kriging is a desirable interpolator in that it follows prescribed values at pilot-point locations, and among other desirable characteristics, provides best linear unbiased estimates of hydraulic property values between interpolation points (pilot points in our case). Some of its benefits may be overstated (Philip and Watson, 1986), however, especially if only a small subset of pilot points is used in interpolating to any one model grid or cell. This creates discontinuities in the interpolation scheme at those locations where a point is added or removed, thus compromising not only its claims to best linear unbiased estimation, but also possibly to satisfaction of equation 29. Another drawback of Kriging in the present context is that it is not an orthogonal interpolator.

This section is completed with an interesting property of Kriging as an interpolator.

k is a random vector representing, for example, hydraulic properties assigned to model cells throughout a model domain. It is partitioned into two subvectors such that

$$\mathbf{k}^T = [\mathbf{k}_1\ \mathbf{k}_2]^T , \tag{79}$$

where, for example, $\mathbf{k}_2$ is a subvector of pilot-point locations collocated with model cell centers, and $\mathbf{k}_1$ is the subvector of the remaining cell centers.

The covariance matrix **C**(**k**) of **k** is partitioned accordingly as

$$C(\mathbf{k}) = \begin{bmatrix} \mathbf{C}_{11} & \mathbf{C}_{12} \\ \mathbf{C}_{21} & \mathbf{C}_{22} \end{bmatrix} , \tag{80}$$

where $\mathbf{C}_{11}$ and $\mathbf{C}_{22}$ are the covariance matrices of $\mathbf{k}_1$ and $\mathbf{k}_2$, respectively, and $\mathbf{C}_{12} = \mathbf{C}_{21}$ is the cross-covariance matrix between $\mathbf{k}_1$ and $\mathbf{k}_2$.

Suppose that the elements comprising $\mathbf{k}_2$ become known through estimation of the pilot-point values in the calibration process. Then, if **k** follows a multi-Gaussian distribution, the conditional expectation of the remaining elements of **k**, these comprising $\mathbf{k}_1$, can be computed as

$$E(\mathbf{k}_1|\mathbf{k}_2) = \mathbf{C}_{12}\mathbf{C}_{22}^{-1}\mathbf{k}_2 . \tag{81}$$

This is the same equation as used by the "simple Kriging" interpolation scheme.

The conditional covariance matrix of $\mathbf{k}_1$ is

$$C(\mathbf{k}_1) = \mathbf{C}_{12}\mathbf{C}_{22}^{-1}\mathbf{C}_{21} . \tag{82}$$

With some manipulation, it can be shown that $E(\mathbf{k}_1 | \mathbf{k}_2)$ also can be calculated as

$$E(\mathbf{k}_1|\mathbf{k}_2) = -\mathbf{D}_{11}^{-1}\mathbf{D}_{12}\mathbf{k}_2 \tag{83}$$

where

$$\mathbf{D} = \begin{bmatrix} \mathbf{D}_{11} & \mathbf{D}_{12} \\ \mathbf{D}_{21} & \mathbf{D}_{22} \end{bmatrix} = \begin{bmatrix} \mathbf{C}_{11} & \mathbf{C}_{12} \\ \mathbf{C}_{21} & \mathbf{C}_{22} \end{bmatrix}^{-1} . \tag{84}$$

It also can be shown that where $\mathbf{k}_1$ is computed from $\mathbf{k}_2$ in this manner, then

$$\mathbf{k}^T C^{-1}(\mathbf{k})\mathbf{k} = \mathbf{k}^T D(\mathbf{k})\mathbf{k} = \mathbf{k}_2^T \mathbf{C}_{22}^{-1}\mathbf{k}_2 . \tag{85}$$

This shows that if we have calculated a hydraulic property field for a model domain by Kriging from a set of pilot points, the geological likelihood function for that entire field can be computed simply through calculating the likelihood function pertaining to the pilot points.

This appears to indicate that a maximum likelihood solution to the inverse problem can be obtained by applying Tikhonov regularization to an arbitrary set of pilot-point parameters from which computation of grid parameter values is accomplished through Kriging (as is often done in practice). It must not be forgotten, however, that equation 85 does not indicate that Kriging is the optimal interpolation method for use in an inversion context. It states that if Kriging is used for computation of cell-based parameter values from pilot-point parameter values, then computation of the geological component of the parameter likelihood function (through which parameter likelihood is assessed in terms of the C(**k**) matrix of innate parameter spatial variability) is a computationally simple matter.

Background and Issues Regarding Use of Pilot Points

The purpose of this section is to make use of insights gained through the mathematical explorations of the previous section, which lead to recommendations for the most effective use of pilot points in calibration of an environmental model. First, it is necessary to identify the aim of the calibration process and thereby establish the metric by which any recommendations on any aspect of that process can be judged:

First, we seek values for parameters, and predictions dependent upon them, that are "expected" in the statistical sense, and (or) that approach "maximum likelihood." As Moore and Doherty (2006) point out, this does not mean that model predictions made based on the calibrated parameter set are necessarily "right" or even "likely;" only that their potential for wrongness has been minimized. Neither does it mean that the potential for wrongness is necessarily small–only that it is roughly symmetrically disposed about the parameter set that we take to be the "calibrated parameter set." As a result, the (manual or mathematical) regularization process required to achieve a unique (and optimal) solution to the poorly posed inverse problem normally requires that the calibrated parameter field assigned to a model be a simplified version of reality, comprising only those aspects of reality that can be estimated with integrity, based on what is known about the system.

The use of a reduced parameter set based on pilot points is a numerical convenience, developed out of the necessity to reduce the number of parameters requiring estimation to those for which derivatives can be computed in a reasonable amount of time. In most cases of current model usage, these derivatives are computed through finite differencing, which requires at least one forward model run per parameter. Where alternative means of derivatives calculation are available, for example through the use of adjoint-state methods (for example, using MODFLOW-2005, Clemo, written communication, 2007), the necessity to use a reduced parameter set may be reduced or even eliminated for some problems.

Unfortunately, use of a reduced parameter set requires that compromises be made and that the performance of the calibration process as judged according to the above metric is therefore diminished. Normally, however, it is not the fit between model outcomes and field measurements that is affected. It generally is not too difficult to define a reduced parameter set with proper mathematical regularization that provides an adequate fit between model outputs and field measurements, given the expected measurement/structural noise contained in the measurement dataset. The challenge, rather, is ensuring that the parameter field is indeed that of maximum likelihood or minimum error variance (which we assume herein are essentially equivalent), so that *predictions* calculated based on this parameter set can claim the same property.

Computation of parameter and predictive error intervals is beyond the scope of this report but salient aspects are briefly described below. Tonkin and Doherty (2009) describe calibration-constrained Monte-Carlo analysis, which can be carried out with a high level of efficiency following calibration of a pilot-point-parameterized model using regularized inversion. Such an analysis uses the calibrated field as its starting point. Differences between randomly generated parameter sets (at the **k** level of detail) and the calibrated field are computed prior to projection of these differences into the calibration null space. The projected differences are then added back onto the calibrated parameter field as initial estimates for use in a pilot-point-based recalibration process. The advantages of this method as a measure of parameter and predictive uncertainty are dependent upon the integrity of the claim of the calibrated parameter field to be one of maximum likelihood. The method commonly demonstrates a wide range of variability for many model predictions, notwithstanding the calibration constraints on parameter fields used by the model. In most cases, errors introduced to the calibration/uncertainty analysis process through use of a reduced parameter set are small in comparison to the post-calibration uncertainty resulting from the nonuniqueness of solution of the inverse problem.

Practical Considerations

Compromises involved in the use of a reduced parameter set are just one of the many compromises that are made in building and calibrating a groundwater model. A few of the shortcomings of the model construction and calibration process are relevant here.

Calculation of Derivatives

There are a number of repercussions developed out of the necessity to calculate derivatives as is commonly done using finite differences. These include the following:

1. The upper limit on the number of pilot points that can be used in the parameter-estimation process is often set by a modeler's access to computer resources. Notwithstanding the fact that the burden of lengthy model run times can be dramatically reduced through parallelization of model runs and through use of the SVD-assist inversion engine (Tonkin and Doherty, 2005), this facet of model design often sets an upper limit on the number of parameters used in the inversion process. Cloud computing may address these shortcomings to some extent (Hunt and others, 2010), but currently the guidelines presented herein are best viewed as "making the best of a bad situation," in which compromises will be inevitable but whose detrimental effects can be minimized.

2. Model numerical behavior (particularly the numerical behavior of complex models) often contains granularity and thresholds. Poor convergence of numerical solution schemes, the occurrence of MODFLOW dry cells, and adaptive time stepping used by many transport and groundwater/surface water interaction models, can compromise derivatives of model outputs with respect to adjustable parameters. Although a gradient-based parameter-estimation process is somewhat resilient to numerical artifacts, its performance is not expected to be optimal. Furthermore, the greater the number of parameters for which estimates are sought, the greater the detrimental effects inflicted by poor performance of the model are on the parameter-estimation process.

3. As the number of parameters grows, the sensitivity of individual parameters diminishes. This, in turn, introduces errors to finite-difference derivatives as smaller numbers that are close together are subtracted, losing numerical significance in the process.

Structural Noise

Although commonly referred to as "measurement noise," much of a model's inability to simulate the complex natural world is actually "structural noise" that arises from the imperfect nature of the simplified model. Some structural noise arises from parameter simplification that is an indispensable aspect of model calibration whether achieved through mathematical regularization or manual means. Using methods such as those developed by Cooley (2004), the structural noise from manual simplification can be accommodated to some extent in the inversion process to more closely approach maximum likelihood of estimated parameter fields; however, this is rarely done in practice as it is a numerically burdensome procedure and pertains only to structural noise induced by a given parameter simplification scheme (that is, a new simplification scheme requires the entire analysis be re-run).

Structural noise shows a high degree of temporal and spatial correlation—a correlation structure that (especially for that induced by model imperfections) cannot be accommodated through selection of a weight matrix that is proportional to its inverse—for neither its correlation structure nor its inverse is known. Lack of knowledge of both the magnitude of structural noise, and of its correlation structure, compromises the extent to which a parameter field can be declared to be of maximum likelihood or of minimum error variance (Doherty and Welter, 2010).

Spatial Covariance Matrix

The central role of the covariance matrix of spatial parameter variability ($C(\mathbf{k})$) in consideration of native or reduced model parameterization is apparent from the discussion of the previous section. This matrix generally is not even approximately known, even where direct measurements of hydraulic properties have been made at a number of locations and (or) where knowledge of local geology is good. Furthermore, hydraulic properties rarely are likely to exhibit statistical stationarity and are even less likely to be Gaussian. In addition, inferring even the magnitude of its diagonal terms through the calibration process is fraught with difficulty owing to its interplay with the $C(\varepsilon)$ matrix of measurement/structural noise. Acceptance of a high degree of spatial variation in a calibrated parameter field often means acceptance of a high degree of model-to-measurement fit, and therefore of a low magnitude $C(\varepsilon)$, and vice versa.

Number and Placement of Pilot Points

Advantages of deploying pilot points on a uniform grid include the following:

1. The relation between pilot point spatial density and parameter field spatial frequencies admitted to the calibration process is readily apparent.

2. More flexibility is available in the design of interpolation functions, especially those that seek orthogonality.

3. If pre- or post-calibration analyses based on members of the PEST GENLINPRED utility suite (Doherty, 2010) are to be undertaken to determine contributions made by different parameter types to the uncertainty of model predictions, spurious inflation of parameter contributions as a result of nonuniform spatial pilot-point density is avoided.

4. The potential to introduce artificialities such as "bulls-eyes" into a calibrated parameter field is diminished, for no area within the model domain is in a "pilot-point desert," containing isolated pilot points far from the others. Such an occurrence can result in incorrect parameterization both within the "desert" itself, and in locations close to the "desert," where pilot-point parameters may be given unrealistically high or low values (especially if unconstrained by measurements) to introduce heterogeneity to parts of the model domain where excessive separation denies them leverage.

5. Use of a regular network of pilot points generally is more objective than use of an irregular network, thus avoiding decisions regarding local pilot-point density and placement.

Advantages of irregular pilot-point distribution include the following:

1. Irregular pilot-point emplacement can be more computationally efficient. Thus, more pilot points can be placed in regions of high data density and less can be placed in regions of low data density.

2. Pilot points can be placed at the locations of wells at which pumping tests have been performed; parameter values assigned to these points can reflect the outcomes of those tests.

3. Pilot-point placement can be optimized with respect to measurement point locations. For example, studies of post-calibration resolution matrices indicate that the averaging kernels that express the relations between parameter hydraulic conductivity fields assigned to calibrated models and those that exist in reality have highest values at locations between wells along streamlines that separate them. Placement of pilot points at these locations would help to ensure that the resolution matrix produced as an outcome of the reduced-parameter calibration process is as diagonally dominant as possible (this reducing the effect of the "**I** – **R**" or "null space term" on parameter and predictive error variance; Moore and Doherty, 2005). Similarly, where pilot points are used for parameterization of storage coefficient, optimality of reduced-parameter resolution matrices can be approached if pilot points are placed at the sites of wells in which water table variations were measured.

4. In places where hydraulic properties are known to show high spatial variability or can be inferred to exhibit this variability (for example, where piezometric contours show locally steep gradients), pilot points can be placed at locations where they are able to best "capture" this variability through the calibration process.

5. It is widely documented that the information content of concentration measurements for estimating local hydraulic conductivity is far greater than that of head measurements. When calibrating a contaminant transport model against a dataset that includes historical concentration measurements, it would be more advantageous to have a higher pilot-point density within, rather than outside, a contaminant plume.

6. Emplacement of pilot points with high spatial density near locations where predictions are to be made (especially predictions such as contaminant fate that are particularly sensitive to spatial hydraulic property variability) enhances the capacity of post-calibration predictive uncertainty analysis to compute the true uncertainty associated with these predictions as the null space contribution to their uncertainty is thereby more reliably calculated.

The approaches for pilot-point placement do not need to be mutually exclusive. A combined approach starts with a regularly spaced grid of pilot points that is then refined with additional pilot points in areas of interest or containing many observations. Regardless of whether pilot-point placement is at regular or irregular intervals, the primary concern in either case is whether enough of them are deployed to ensure that differences between **j** and **k** lie in the null-space of **Z** (that is, that equation 29 is satisfied). Through violation of this condition, the use of too few pilot points, can compromise the ability of the calibration process to obtain as good a fit between model outputs and field data as is supported by the level of noise associated with the data. Furthermore, it can compromise optimality of the calibration process by introducing spurious local parameter values, either because insufficient data density disallows introduction of local heterogeneity that is warranted by the data or because pilot points are not placed at the exact locations where such heterogeneity can be inferred to exist. In many contexts, this provides a strong case for use of an irregular pilot-point network so that high density requirements at one location within a model domain do not then require that the same density prevail over the entirety of that model domain.

Pilot-Point Density

Where a calibration process involves multiple parameter families (for example, hydraulic properties of different types in the same layer or of the same type in different layers), it is not necessary that the same density be used for all parameter families. For example, the conductance of an aquitard often is poorly resolved by measurement data; therefore, a relatively low pilot-point density may be sufficient to satisfy equation 29 for this parameter type. Similarly, the density of pilot points in areas of high hydraulic conductivity can be lower than in areas of low hydraulic conductivity owing to the greater resolving power of head measurements in the latter areas.

There may be some calibration contexts where pilot-point density is strategically used by the modeler as an improvised regularization device. The link between pilot-point spacing and spatial frequencies that are capable of representation in a calibrated hydraulic property field was discussed above. Pilot-point density can thus be used by a modeler as a means of restricting the introduction of heterogeneity at a scale that is considered too small to be geologically reasonable. As the above discussion shows, the highest spatial frequency that can be represented in a pilot-point based field is half the spatial frequency of pilot-point emplacement.

The use of Tikhonov regularization also can limit the extent to which local heterogeneity is introduced to a pilot-point-based calibration process. Use of Tikhonov regularization can therefore allow a modeler to safely use higher pilot-point densities than would otherwise be tractable. This can be useful in many calibration circumstances because, in general, the more pilot points that are used, the smaller are the chances that any one point will be assigned an incorrect value through being placed at a less-than-optimal position with respect to local heterogeneity that manifests itself through the calibration process. On the other hand, if the calibration process irregularly applies Tikhonov regularization constraints by assigning diminished weights to these constraints to achieve a worthy fit in some parts of the model domain where both data density and heterogeneity are high, its stabilizing effects in other parts of the model domain, where data density may be much lower, can be lost. This then may result in the introduction of spurious heterogeneity where pilot-point density is high in data-poor areas. In many modeling contexts, however, it may be possible to at least partially overcome this problem through use of subspace-enhanced Tikhonov constraints (see the Current Research section later in this report).

Interpolation

Pilot Points and Zones

Software provided with the PEST Groundwater Data Utility suite (Doherty, 2007) allows the use of pilot points to be combined with that of zones. Thus, pilot-point parameters used in the calibration process can be grouped into zone-specific sets of parameters. This ensures that interpolation does not cross zone boundaries; therefore, the modeler is free to enforce hydraulic property discontinuities at these boundaries. Presumably, use of zones in conjunction with pilot points will be accompanied by a regularization scheme that encourages the introduction of discontinuous heterogeneity at the boundaries of zones in preference to continuously between intra-zonal pilot points. Although this topic is beyond the scope of this report, the issue of a suitable regularization methodology is not trivial. If zones are few enough and data are plentiful enough for the zones to act as both regularization devices and parameterization devices, then regularization as it pertains to zones is not needed. If the use of zones with boundaries impervious to interpolation from points outside of each zone creates nonuniqueness in solution of the inverse problem, then regularization is required. Tikhonov regularization may not be necessary; a form of subspace regularization, such as SVD-assisted solution of the inverse problem, may suffice.

Although the use of pilot points in conjunction with zones will not be discussed further and much of the discussion that follows addresses cases where pilot points are used pervasively throughout a model domain, this need not be the case. Pilot points may be assigned to a single zone within a model domain composed of multiple zones, or they may be deployed separately and independently in many different zones. Finally, the software supplied with the PEST Groundwater Data Utility suite allows a zone to be populated by a single pilot point. In this case, the hydraulic property assigned to the pilot point applies to the whole zone, and the pilot-point parameter becomes a de facto zonal parameter.

Kriging

Currently, utilities available as part of the PEST Groundwater Data Utility suite support only the use of Kriging for spatial interpolation between pilot points and a model mesh or grid. Use of Kriging has the following advantages:

1. Kriging honors data values at interpolation points.
2. Interpolation coefficients are calculated easily.
3. They can be calculated prior to the parameter-estimation process so that interpolation consumes minimal computer resources as parameter estimation is performed.
4. In general, it is a smooth interpolator.
5. Anisotropy is introduced easily to the interpolation process, if required.
6. If Tikhonov regularization constraints enforcing maximum likelihood of a cell-based parameter field in terms of an expected variogram are applied directly to pilot points from which that field is interpolated through simple Kriging, the constraints are applied to the entire interpolated field, as discussed above.

The mathematical analysis presented in the previous section has indicated that the use of orthogonal basis functions as an interpolator between pilot points may serve the calibration process better than the use of Kriging. However, Kriging is used widely because of the strengths listed above. Based on experience, suggestions on the implementation of Kriging as an intra-pilot-point interpolation device are as follows.

A variogram for an area is rarely known and heterogeneity is rarely statistically stationary. Therefore, the choice of a variogram as a basis for Kriging often will be made more based on model domain geometry and the distribution of pilot points within the model domain, than based on known or inferred geostatistics of a study area. When choosing a variogram, it is important to recognize that the sill has no effect on how Kriging takes place, unless multiple variogram types are nested to form the one geostatistical structure, and Kriging takes place based on that structure; in that case, only the proportional contributions, rather than the absolute variogram contributions, matter to the Kriging process.

The following strategy has proven successful when choosing variogram properties as a basis for Kriging. Although this strategy may not be suitable in all contexts, it is useful in many models:

1. The exponential variogram type often performs better than the spherical, Gaussian, or power variogram types, as this type appears to be least prone to the creation of spurious parameter fields between closely spaced pilot points of very different value. The introduction of such locally spurious hydraulic properties can degrade greatly claims of maximum likelihood for a calibrated model parameter field. The equation for the exponential variogram ($\gamma(h)$)is

$$\gamma(h) = C_0[1 - \exp(-h/a)] \tag{86}$$

   where C_0 is the sill of the variogram, h is the absolute value of separation distance between points, and a determines its range. Where pilot points are distributed non-uniformly throughout a model domain, choose a value for a that is about equal to the largest cell-to-pilot-point distance over which interpolation must take place. That is, choose it to be about equal to the greatest distance by which any model cell is separated from a pilot point. For uniformly spaced pilot points, choose a to be between one and two pilot-point separation distances.

2. Specify an infinite interpolation search radius.

3. Despite the infinite search radius, limit the number of pilot points used in the interpolation process to between 5 and 10. This allows local heterogeneity to express itself in the calibration process by the assignment of values to pilot points that exist only near where the data indicates that this heterogeneity exists. Allowing distant points, even though suppressed by the variogram, to influence local heterogeneity can result in over-smoothing of the calibrated parameter field.

4. Introduce anisotropy to the variogram according to geological expectations of directions of preferential continuity of anomalous hydraulic property features.

The third point above is important for more than one reason. First, it mitigates the possibility of spurious values being assigned to Kriged parameter fields near identified hydraulic property heterogeneities. Second, if as is often the case, parameters need to assume abnormal values to become surrogates for features or processes that are unrepresented in a model, the "collateral damage" of their having to do this is limited to the near vicinity of the feature or process that causes the problem. Commonly, this can lead to more rapid identification (and sometimes rectification) of model inadequacies than would be the case if the effects of the model's inadequacies had to be spread over a broader part of the model domain. On other occasions, it simply limits the damage done by model imperfections. Third, as the radius of influence of each pilot point is reduced, the Kriging interpolation scheme approaches orthogonality. In the limit, when each cell is influenced by only one pilot point, a nearest-neighbor scheme is used. As discussed above, this indeed is an orthogonal interpolation scheme.

The final of the previous four points also is important. Pursuit of a maximum likelihood parameter field requires not only that heterogeneity be suppressed unless supported by the calibration dataset, it also requires that where it is introduced, this is done in a manner that is geologically reasonable. In many geological contexts, this will require that features possess a tendency for elongation in one direction but not in another.

An Orthogonal Interpolator

The mathematical analyses of the previous sections demonstrate the benefits to be accrued through implementation of an orthogonal interpolation scheme from pilot points to the model grid or mesh. Interpolation functions can be viewed as basis functions. The use of orthogonal interpolators can thus be viewed as the use of an orthogonal set of basis functions, each with a value of one at the pilot point with which it is associated, and with a value of zero at all other pilot points, for reasons discussed above.

At present, pilot-point functionality provided with the PEST Groundwater Data Utilities suite (Doherty, 2007) provides no option for orthogonal interpolation. This is a subject of ongoing research, which is discussed further in the Future Research section of this report.

Regularization

Pilot Points as a Regularization Device

As discussed above, the use of a reduced parameter set can be considered as a regularization device in its own right in that it prevents the occurrence of heterogeneity at too fine a scale. Where the reduced parameter set is composed of pilot points, and where **L** in equation 14 thus constitutes an interpolator, it can prevent the introduction to the calibrated parameter field of hydraulic property variations whose spatial frequency is greater than half that of the pilot-point emplacement frequency.

Suppose that pilot points were used without simultaneous use of Tikhonov regularization. Suppose also that a maximum likelihood solution to the inverse problem was sought based on no spatial correlation existing between these points, and that they are thus statistically independent of each other. As figure 4 shows, the interpolated parameter field would indeed possess spatial correlation because spatial frequencies beyond half the pilot-point emplacement frequency cannot exist within this field. Although it may not be possible to encapsulate this stochastic description of spatial variability using one of the standard variogram equations, under some circumstances it may nevertheless constitute an adequate enough description of geological variability to estimate geologically reasonable fields from the calibration process. Use of a variogram to describe spatial heterogeneity relations is more a convenience than anything else and (especially in water-resource studies) is seldom based on detailed geostatistical analysis. Furthermore, even if a geostatistical study had been undertaken, the choice of one variogram over another is often subjective.

In some circumstances, the use of pilot points alone, with no simultaneous Tikhonov regularization, may form a suitable basis for both parameterization and "first-order regularization" of a groundwater model. The pilot-point spatial emplacement frequency should be such that parameterization spatial frequencies above half this level should lie within the calibration null space, according to equation 64. Meanwhile, the variability associated with spatial frequencies below this would be expected to be constant with respect to spatial frequency, as is depicted in the lower two panels of figure 5. The words "first order" are used above because mathematical regularization then will be required in solution of the inverse problem of assigning values to pilot points; however, this can take the form of SVD alone, with no other form of regularization required, owing to the presumed statistical independence of the pilot-point parameters.

To examine this in a little more detail, suppose that pilot points **p** possess a spatial covariance matrix C(**p**) described by

$$C(\mathbf{p}) = \sigma_{\mathrm{p}}^2\mathbf{I} \quad (87)$$

From equation 14, model parameterization **j** on a cell-by-cell basis then has a spatial covariance matrix given by

$$C(\mathbf{j}) = \sigma_{\mathrm{p}}^2\mathbf{L}\mathbf{L}^T . \quad (88)$$

This is of diminished rank, and therefore contains many singular values of magnitude zero (which is why it lacks capacity to represent high spatial frequencies). If **L** is an orthogonal interpolator, its columns represent the eigenvectors of C(**j**). Where **L** is not orthogonal, this is not the case. In this case, suppose that (through singular value decomposition)

$$\mathbf{L}\mathbf{L}^T = \mathbf{U}\mathbf{S}\mathbf{U}^T \quad (89)$$

(where **S** includes zero-valued singular values because of the column-rank-deficiency of **L**). Then C(**j**) becomes

$$C(\mathbf{j}) = \sigma_{\mathrm{p}}^2\mathbf{U}\mathbf{S}\mathbf{U}^T . \quad (90)$$

The question of whether certain pilot-point spacings used in conjunction with certain interpolation functions can achieve desirable properties for C(**j**) is addressed in the section on future directions, as this is a matter that requires investigation both into what properties it is desirable for this interpolator to possess, and whether these can be achieved or approximately achieved, through choice of a particular **L**.

Meanwhile, for guidance based on present knowledge, there may be situations where regularization inherent in the use of pilot points itself may be turned to advantage in certain geological contexts. In particular, where spatial correlation of geological features is unlikely to exist over a distance greater than the separation of pilot points, then their use in conjunction with SVD as a device for solution of the inverse problem may lead to something approaching a maximum likelihood solution for that problem. Although this may be viewed as a geologically unlikely situation, it may not be the case when combined with anisotropic interpolation. The existence of elongated anomalous features of limited width that may terminate relatively abruptly may indeed be a suitable geological abstraction to use for the purpose of model parameterization in some geological contexts.

Tikhonov Regularization

As was discussed in the "Theory" section of this report, if spatial variability of hydraulic properties **k** is characterized by a spatial covariance matrix C(**k**), then the pursuit of a maximum likelihood solution to the inverse problem dictates that estimates be made of the coefficients by which the eigenvectors of this matrix are multiplied after normalization with respect to the standard deviation of variability associated with each such eigenvector; these are the elements of the matrix **m** of equation 33. This is not practical in real-world groundwater-model calibration, however, because:

1. C(**k**) is rarely known.
2. There probably is not much point in "knowing" C(**k**), as it is unlikely to provide an adequate description of innate hydraulic property spatial variability.
3. In most model domains, hydraulic property spatial variability is unlikely even to be stationary.

Furthermore, computation of basis functions corresponding to the eigenvectors of C(**k**) over a densely gridded or meshed model domain would be a computationally burdensome procedure. (It is possible that the LSQR solver of Paige and Saunders (1982) or the PROPACK solver of Larsen (1998) may afford good approximations.)

In light of these difficulties, the question arises whether model calibration should attempt to estimate the normalized eigencomponents of C(**p**), the covariance matrix of a reduced parameter set, rather than those of C(**k**). In the present context, the reduced parameter set would be composed of hydraulic property values assigned to pilot points. The covariance matrix of C(**p**) is related to that of C(**k**) through the relation

$$C(\mathbf{p}) = \mathbf{N}C(\mathbf{k})\mathbf{N}^T \quad (91)$$

where

$$\mathbf{N} = \mathbf{L}. \quad (92)$$

As discussed previously, unless **L** is orthogonal, **N** generally cannot be determined. In contrast, if **L** satisfies equation 46 and/or 48, **N** can be determined uniquely, so that (after equation 68)

$$C(\mathbf{p}) = \alpha^2 \mathbf{L}^T C(\mathbf{k})\mathbf{L}. \quad (93)$$

Note, however, that where **L** is non-orthogonal, **N** could be inferred using a formula such as equation 20, which is repeated here for convenience:

$$\mathbf{N} = (\mathbf{L}^T\mathbf{L})^{-1}\mathbf{L}. \quad (94)$$

Furthermore, if pilot points are close enough together, then considering the approximations made in assuming a given C(**k**) in the first place, C(**p**) could be equated roughly to

$$C(\mathbf{p}) = \mathbf{S}C(\mathbf{k})\mathbf{S}^T \quad (95)$$

where **S** is simply a selection matrix that selects elements from C(**k**) that pertain to model grid cells that coincide with pilot-point locations.

For the same reasons as outlined above (particularly that of lack of stationarity of most realistic hydraulic property fields), estimation of normalized eigencomponents of C(**p**) probably would not provide a practical means of groundwater-model calibration in most instances. Nevertheless, the fact that even an approximate C(**p**) or C(**k**) matrix exists should not be ignored in seeking an optimal solution to the inverse problem. In fact, it is impossible *not* to make some assumption about the innate variability of subsurface hydraulic properties. For example, if the minimum norm solution to the inverse problem is sought at the **k** level through computation of $\underline{\mathbf{k}}$ using SVD, implied in this choice of solution method is the fact that C(**k**) is assumed to be equal to $\delta_k^2\mathbf{I}$. If the minimum norm solution is sought at the pilot-point level (through SVD-based computation of $\underline{\mathbf{p}}$), this assumes variability of **k** in ways that are discussed above.

Therefore, there can be no consideration of obtaining a maximum likelihood solution to the inverse problem unless we explicitly take C(**k**) into account, even if it is known only approximately. SVD-estimation of normalized eigencomponents of this matrix has been shown to be infeasible. Use of Tikhonov regularization presents a practical alternative; however, whether this is applied at the level of native hydraulic parameters **k** or at the level of the reduced parameter set **p**, its usefulness is based on the following characteristics:

1. A modeler does not need to be as "committed" to a particular C(**k**) when using that matrix as part of a Tikhonov scheme as when choosing to estimate the normalized eigencomponents of this matrix. When embodying C(**k**) in a Tikhonov regularization scheme, the user designates that should it be necessary for local heterogeneity to arise, this should occur in a certain manner with certain preferred continuity relations followed to the extent feasible.

2. When applied in conjunction with an inverse problem solution algorithm such as that used by PEST, where the regularization weight factor is adjusted to complement a user-supplied target measurement objective function selected based on the anticipated level of measurement/structural noise, the strength with which Tikhonov constraints are applied can be adjusted automatically as the parameter-estimation process progresses. Selection of a less-than-perfect C(**k**) then can be complemented by a reduction in the strength with which regularization is applied, if its application compromises model-to-measurement fit.

"Preferred-Value" Regularization

The easiest to way to implement Tikhonov regularization is to provide a single item of prior information for each parameter used in the parameter-estimation process. In each such equation, that parameter is equated to its pre-calibration maximum likelihood value (which also should be its initial value). In geophysics, this is referred to as a smallness model or minimum-norm regularization (Aster and others, 2005 for example). A covariance matrix then is assigned to all of these prior information equations according to the statistics of parameter spatial variability; this is the C(**p**) matrix, derived as above from the C(**k**) matrix, so that it pertains to the reduced parameter set. Where measurement noise is small, this formulation of the inverse problem approaches that described by equation 52, and thus achieves maximum likelihood.

Use of preferred-value regularization has the following advantages:

1. It is easy to implement (see below).

2. It requires only one prior information equation per parameter. If a single, non-diagonal, C(**p**) covariance matrix is supplied in conjunction with all of these prior information equations, then for most parameter-estimation problems groundwater modelers encounter, inversion of this matrix for use in equation 52 is not too numerically laborious of a task.

3. In multi-layer contexts, preferred-value regularization can be applied to each layer and to each parameter type separately, possibly with separate C(**p**) submatrices for each. Inversion of a composite block diagonal C(**p**) matrix such as this should present no numerical difficulties.

4. If point measurements of hydraulic properties are available (for example, through pumping test analyses), the preferred value at each pilot-point location can be computed through Kriging from pumping test sites to the locations of pilot points. Furthermore, the covariance matrix of spatial variability C(**p**) can be altered in accordance with the conditioning effect of direct acquisition of system properties at pumping test locations. Thus, maximum use is made of site characterization data in seeking a maximum likelihood calibration of the model.

The principal disadvantage of preferred-value regularization, however, is the fact that there are many situations where a preferred value for hydraulic properties is not known. Therefore, as the regularization weight factor is reduced to achieve a desired fit with the data (as it must be if preferred parameter values are mis-assigned), numerical stability is lost from the inversion process and parameter estimation may falter as a result.

The choice of an appropriate C(**p**) matrix to use was discussed in the previous section. Though it is not strictly theoretically correct, given the uncertainty associated with selection of a C(**k**) matrix, little is lost by computing C(**p**) based on the same variogram as that used for C(**k**) (thus by using equation 95).

Ideally, for reasons discussed earlier in this report, an orthogonal interpolator should be used to calculate hydraulic property values for the cells of a model grid or mesh from those assigned to pilot points. Presently, PEST groundwater modeling utility support software does not provide such an interpolator. Non-orthogonal interpolation may yet be beneficial, however, if its use results in an interpolated parameter field that has certain desirable relations with the assumed C(**k**) matrix of hydraulic property spatial variability.

"Preferred Difference" Regularization

Although specific preferred differences can be specified, regularization constraints often are supplied in the form of "preferred homogeneity," where the preferred parameter difference value is zero. Imposition of constraints of this type can lead to "smooth" solutions to the inverse problem. This may be more appropriate than preferred-value regularization where heterogeneity arises in a meaningful way out of a smooth condition, and a preferred background value is not known.

These techniques often are described in geophysics as higher-order Tikhonov regularization (Aster and others, 2005), which use a "smoothness" function in the form of a first- or second-derivative function imposed on the parameter field.

PEST utilities support pilot-point-based preferred difference regularization in which prior information equations that encapsulate these differences are assigned weights that decrease with increasing pilot-point separation, in accordance with the presumed hydraulic property variogram for a study site. Each pilot point is linked to a number of other pilot points using a single difference equation for each such linkage, the number of such linkages being set by the user.

This scheme has a number of disadvantages and could be considered in need of improvement. These disadvantages include the following:

1. It results in a large number of prior information equations as each pilot-point difference requires its own equation. This is not necessarily a problem, but it does require efficient internal storage of the resulting Jacobian matrix.

2. It ignores the fact that parameter differences are in fact statistically correlated. For example, **T** is a (large) matrix (with many columns) that expresses these difference relations. The covariance matrix of the set of "observed" differences of zero, which collectively make up preferred difference regularization constraints used in a calibration process, is actually given by

$$C(\mathbf{t}) = \mathbf{T}C(\mathbf{p})\mathbf{T}^T \tag{96}$$

where $\mathbf{t} = \mathbf{Tp}$.

Where each pilot point is linked to many other pilot points, use of this covariance matrix in the inversion process would be impractical because of its large size, in spite of the fact that pilot points constitute a reduced parameter set with respect to the native model parameters **k**.

In spite of its shortcomings, the method presently supported by the PEST Groundwater Data Utilities has proven to be a successful regularization device in many practical inversion settings. Use of a C(**p**) matrix, calculated according to the same variogram as C(**k**), makes the method easy to implement. Furthermore, its theoretical shortcomings probably do not compromise the mathematical integrity of the parameter-estimation process any more than do the many other approximations that are involved in this process, some of which were discussed previously.

Other Regularization Formulations

The geophysical literature discusses the use of nonlinear Tikhonov relations that can be used for purposes such as:

1. To enhance the ability of heterogeneity to arise in a spatially limited manner whereby "total heterogeneity mass" is of maximum spatial density, rather than being diffuse.
2. To enhance the ability for heterogeneity to arise in proximity to known or inferred geological bodies.
3. To promote maximum adherence to certain shapes/dispositions/orientations of any heterogeneity that arises through the inversion process.
4. Using maximum entropy to enforce adherence to a weighted preferred value without penalizing sharp peaks and enforcing non-negativity through log transformation.

See, for example, Portniaguine and Zhdanov (1999) and Aster and others (2005) for discussion of some of these types of regularization.

PEST is able to accommodate nonlinear regularization relations just as easily as it accommodates linear regularization relations in the Tikhonov regularization process formulated as the constrained minimization problem of equation 53. These methods offer exciting possibilities for useful deployment in the groundwater-modeling context. However, there is currently no software available to assist in the automatic construction of these nonlinear regularization constraints.

Presently Available Software

The PEST Groundwater Data Utilities include a suite of programs that facilitate the use of pilot-point parameterization in the groundwater-modeling context. Some of these programs include the ability to generate "preferred difference" prior information equations simultaneously with the computation of Kriging factors. The most powerful means of adding linear regularization constraints to a PEST-based inverse problem is provided by the GENREG utility. This utility has the ability to write prior information equations that link parameters within and between hydrostratigraphic units according to relations that may or may not involve parameter spatial location, with weight assignment strategies that may or may not involve a parameter covariance matrix. See Doherty (2007) for more details.

Within the PEST suite itself, the ADDREG1 utility provides the easiest means of adding "preferred value" linear regularization to any PEST input dataset. This adds a prior information equation for each adjustable parameter to the PEST control file, in which that parameter is equated to its initial value. Prior information equations are assigned to different regularization groups according to the parameters they cite; PEST is able to assign differential weighting to these groups in inverse proportion to the composite sensitivities of parameters they cite.

Summary of Using Tikhonov Regularization with Pilot Points

In most incidences of underdetermined pilot-point-based parameter estimation, it is recommended that Tikhonov regularization be used, regardless of whether other regularization devices such as SVD or SVD-assisted inversion also are used. Practical experience has demonstrated that parameter fields computed using an inversion scheme that includes Tikhonov regularization are more geologically reasonable than those that do not, even with simultaneous use of subspace regularization. The type of regularization best used is context-specific; it is anticipated that the previous discussion, as well as the discussion below, will assist a modeler in selecting an appropriate scheme for a particular modeling context. The use of regularization and SVD-based methods are covered in detail in Doherty and Hunt (2010).

In general, any type of regularization should be "reasonably pervasive." For example, a user may go to great lengths to supply prior information equations, which link pilot-point parameters within each of a number of different hydrostratigraphic units of a model domain, thereby subjecting each layer to comprehensive "difference regularization;" however, they may then neglect to apply regularization between layers. This may result in an ill-posed inverse problem depending on boundary conditions used by the model and observations used in the parameter-estimation process. That is, nonuniqueness may still exist on a layer-by-layer basis as a model may be able to direct water flow through one or another of alternative overlying units with little or no effect on observations. The situation could be rectified in a number of ways. For example, prior information equations specifying interlayer parameter ratios (differences of logged parameter values) could be used. Alternatively, preferred-value regularization could be used for all pilot-point parameters for all layers (or just for some of them). Use of SVD or SVD-assisted inversion also would provide regularization and promote numerical stability by relegating inestimable parameter combinations to the calibration null space.

When undertaking Tikhonov regularization, the user must select a value for the PEST PHIMLIM (target measurement objective function, in equation 53) variable. Fienen and others (2009) suggest this be set to the number of non-zero-weighted observations (where weights are assigned values that are thought to be equal to the inverse of measurement noise standard deviations) because the user is often unaware of the amount of structural noise that is associated with a given dataset. At the beginning of the parameter-estimation process, an alternative approach is to set this variable to a very low value and use the FRACPHIM variable to gain the beneficial effects of Tikhonov regularization as the measurement objective function is lowered. FRACPHIM sets a temporary iteration-specific target measurement objective function at a user-supplied fraction of the current measurement objective function or to the user-supplied value of PHIMLIM, whichever is higher. A value of 0.1 or 0.2 often is most suitable for FRACPHIM. Once an initial parameter-estimation exercise has been carried out, PHIMLIM can be set to a more informed value for subsequent PEST runs. A "useful" value for PHIMLIM is one that provides a good fit between model outputs and field measurements, but shows no signs of over-fitting through exhibiting heterogeneity which is judged to be geologically unreasonable.

If the SVD-assist scheme is used for solution of the inverse problem, PEST can be asked to list each parameter set that results in an improved calibration during subsequent iterations of the overall parameter-estimation process. If parameters achieved at the very end of the parameter-estimation process are judged unrealistic, the user can select a geologically reasonable calibrated parameter set achieved earlier in the parameter-estimation process where the measurement objective function was slightly higher.

To save computation time, PEST ceases execution once the measurement objective falls below PHIMLIM. PEST can, however, be instructed to continue the parameter-estimation process until it is sure that the regularization objective function (which reflects lack of adherence to Tikhonov regularization constraints) is as low as possible (this normally forcing the measurement objective function to rise back to the level of PHIMLIM). When a user desires maximum adherence to the "default parameter conditions" that are encapsulated in regularization constraints, this aspect of PEST functionality should be activated through the control variable REGCONTINUE. Alternatively, PEST could be employed in "pareto" mode to maximize its adherence to regularization constraints; see Doherty, Hunt, and Tonkin (2010) for more information.

See Doherty (2008) for a guide to utility programs supplied with PEST, as well as PEST's capabilities that support use of regularized inversion in the context of groundwater-model calibration.

Solution Methods

PEST provides a number of methods for solution of highly parameterized inverse problems. These include:

1. Gauss-Marquardt-Levenberg with Tikhonov regularization;
2. SVD with or without Tikhonov regularization;
3. SVD-assist with or without Tikhonov regularization; and
4. LSQR with or without Tikhonov regularization.

Where SVD-assist is chosen as a solution device, the user has the option of estimating super parameters using the Gauss-Marquardt-Levenberg, SVD, or LSQR method. Furthermore, when Tikhonov regularization is used, the user has the choice of modifying its application through subspace enhancement, for which a number of implementation options are available.

Although it is beyond the scope of this report to present a description of the strengths and weaknesses of all these alternatives, the following points may guide the selection of pilot-point parameterization schemes and appropriate PEST settings for use in particular modeling contexts:

1. As mentioned previously, Tikhonov regularization should be used in most cases of pilot-point deployment. Furthermore, this should be "reasonably pervasive" in its formulation. If its strength of application appears to diminish toward the end of the parameter-estimation process, and numerical instability results in estimation of unrealistic parameter fields, consider subspace enhancement of Tikhonov regularization.
2. A subspace method should be used for computation of parameter upgrades. When a model runs quickly, SVD should be used. When model run-times are long, SVD-assist may be required instead. Parallelization of model runs can achieve dramatic gains in efficiency in implementing either of these (Hunt and others, 2010).
3. Where SVD-assisted parameter estimation is used, consideration should be given to using SVD as the related solution mechanism for super parameters. This provides "back-up stability" if too many super parameters are specified by the modeler. As described in PEST documentation, use of a few more super parameters than required to achieve uniqueness in solution of the inverse problem, together with Tikhonov regularization, can sometimes provide valuable assistance in overcoming limitations of the SVD-assist methodology when used in conjunction with excessively nonlinear models.

4. If using SVD for solution of the inverse problem (regardless of whether base or super parameters are estimated), a low to intermediate value should be provided for the initial Marquardt lambda (PEST control variable RLAMBDA1); a value of 0.01 to 100 is suitable. The lambda multiplier RLAMFAC then should be set to -2, -3, or -4 to allow wide variation of the Marquardt lambda as the parameter-estimation process progresses. Experience has demonstrated that a wide ranging Marquardt lambda can provide stability in highly nonlinear contexts and can assist in mitigating detrimental effects of poor finite-difference-calculated derivatives.

Current Research Topics

This report is an attempt to commence the process of providing a mathematical description of the role of pilot points in model calibration. It has been assumed that calibration takes place in a highly parameterized context, and that pilot points are used as a practical measure, partly for accommodating the necessity to compute derivatives of model outputs with respect to adjustable parameters using finite parameter differences based on repeated model runs, and partly to reduce other facets of the numerical burden of working in a highly parameterized context such as large computer memory requirements.

The analysis presented herein indicates that pilot-point parameterization and associated regularized inversion, as currently implemented by PEST and its ancillary utility support software, can be extended. Some of the issues that have been identified can be rectified with little effort. On the other hand, some research (probably involving numerical experimentation based on synthetic models) is required before other improvements can be made.

The purpose of this section is to provide some suggestions for improvements to the current methodology and directions for further research into the use of pilot points in highly parameterized regularized inversion. It is possible that some of the suggestions provided below will not, in fact, lead to hoped-for improvements in the use of pilot points as a groundwater-model parameterization device. Nonetheless, the suggested research still will prove worthwhile, for it will have demonstrated that the methods currently applied, although not entirely satisfactory, are as satisfactory as any alternative method.

Subspace Enhanced Tikhonov Regularization

The role of Tikhonov regularization in pilot-point-based inversion has been discussed extensively in this report. It was demonstrated previously that, if used in conjunction with a covariance matrix that provides an appropriate characterization of spatial variability of hydraulic properties, its use converges to the maximum likelihood solution of the inverse problem as measurement noise approaches zero. In the presence of measurement/structural noise of unknown statistical properties, however, no such mathematical guarantee exists. Furthermore, experience in practical implementation of the method has demonstrated less than optimal behavior where hydraulic property heterogeneity and/or measurement/ structural noise are substantial and nonstationary.

Conceptually, it makes sense that regularization constraints should be most strongly applied to those parameters, or to those combinations of parameters, about which the calibration dataset is least informative. At the same time, constraints on those combinations of parameters of which the data is somewhat-to-very informative should not be completely relaxed, for this may lead to over-fitting of that data.

The roles of the calibration solution and null spaces in the parameter-estimation process are described by Moore and Doherty (2005). They show that, within the calibration solution subspace, estimation of eigencomponents of the $Q^{1/2}\mathbf{X}$ matrix (where Q is the observation weight matrix and $\mathbf{X}$ is the Jacobian matrix) associated with singular values of decreasing magnitude is fraught with an increasing likelihood of contamination of these estimates by measurement/structural noise; this potential rises with the inverse of singular value magnitude. This indicates that use of a single regularization weight factor to determine the strength with which all regularization constraints are applied is an inappropriately blunt regularization methodology and that differential weighting of Tikhonov constraints may be more appropriate in many modeling contexts.

As presently implemented, PEST allows some degree of inter-regularization-equation weight factor variability in accordance with the need for strengthened regularization constraints to compensate for observation data inadequacy; this functionality is implemented by setting the IREGADJ regularization control variable to 1, 2, or 3. This strategy is coarse, however, and is based on composite sensitivities of model outputs to individual parameters rather than to linear combinations of parameters (each of which may be individually sensitive but are collectively insensitive because of high correlation).

By setting IREGADJ to 4 or 5, an enhanced form of inter-regularization weights adjustment can be implemented by PEST. This scheme involves projection of all regularization observations and (or) prior information equations onto the eigenvectors of $\mathbf{Q}^{1/2}\mathbf{X}$. A suitable weight for each such regularization constraint then is computed based on the direction cosine between the projection of parameter sensitivities embodied in the constraint and the singular value associated with each eigenvector onto which projection takes place. Testing of the methodology in a variety of practical settings is needed so that suitable guidelines for implementation in various modeling contexts can be identified.

Nonlinear Regularization

The use of nonlinear Tikhonov regularization schemes in facilitating the appearance of geologically realistic heterogeneity through the process of model calibration has been indicated. Such methods may prove very useful in groundwater-model calibration, especially where large regional water-management models are built in data-rich modeling contexts in areas of well-known geology. It follows that the addition of a number of utility programs to the current Groundwater Data Utility suite, which would expedite the use of such methods, would enhance the general utility of the PEST software suite.

Orthogonal Interpolation

The benefits of orthogonal interpolation were discussed previously. In summary, the use of an orthogonal interpolation scheme should provide that parameter field with properties that allow it to approach maximum likelihood status, provided the emplacement density of pilot points is sufficiently high.

This mathematical conclusion is supported by limited practical experience showing that use of a Kriging scheme in which the radius of influence is limited, performs better than one that uses a large search radius. The former scheme more closely approaches orthogonality than the latter scheme.

In an irregular model domain, it may not be possible (or practical) to achieve strict orthogonality of basis or interpolation functions. The problem would be compounded where pilot-point emplacement is irregular, and anisotropy should be introduced to accommodate likely elongation of anomalous features. In fact, an ideal interpolation scheme should be "locally stretchable" (while still maintaining or approaching orthogonality) so that anisotropy can be applied in some areas, but not in others, with a gradation between the two.

The easiest orthogonal interpolation methodology to implement is the nearest-neighbor scheme. In implementing this scheme, each model cell is assigned a value equal to that of its closest pilot point. Although this would indeed achieve orthogonality, it would be more difficult for such a scheme to satisfy equation 29 than a smooth interpolation scheme without the use of an unduly high number of pilot points. It would thus prove difficult to use in conjunction with an irregular pilot-point emplacement strategy, where an attempt is made to complement increased/decreased data density with increased/decreased pilot-point density. It also may lead to the creation of "numerical noise" associated with model predictions made near the boundaries of piecewise orthogonal areas introduced to the model domain through such a scheme. Intuition thus indicates that a smooth interpolator would serve the modeling process better and would provide parameter fields that are more geologically reasonable.

Design of an optimal interpolation scheme to complement pilot-point usage in the groundwater-modeling context is a matter that requires additional research. Apart from orthogonality, other desirable features of such a scheme include the following.

1. It should be easy to apply in complex model domains.
2. Interpolation should be computationally efficient, as it must be undertaken to many thousands (possibly hundreds of thousands) of model cells on many occasions during a typical calibration process.
3. It should be useable with both regular and irregular pilot-point networks.
4. It should readily accommodate (spatially variable) anisotropy.

Other attributes also may be considered desirable for a pilot-point-based interpolation scheme. For example, equation 70 (repeated below) provides the spatial covariance matrix of an interpolated parameter field

$$\mathrm{C}(\mathbf{j}) = \alpha^2\mathbf{LL}^T\mathrm{C}(\mathbf{k})\mathbf{LL}^T = \alpha^2\mathbf{LL}^T\mathbf{WEW}^T\mathbf{LL}^T \,. \quad (97)$$

$\mathrm{C}(\mathbf{j})$ is rank-deficient (because $\mathbf{LL}^T$ is rank-deficient) and thus possesses some (many) zero-valued singular values. If eigenvectors of $\mathrm{C}(\mathbf{j})$ with non-zero singular values approximate the dominate eigenvectors of $\mathrm{C}(\mathbf{k})$, and if the singular values associated with these eigenvectors are similar in both matrices, this gives rise to the situation depicted in the lower panel of figure 6 where an interpolated parameter field retains the same stochastic character as an original field, except for the fact that certain eigencomponents are missing from the interpolated field (hopefully those that span the model's null space in accordance with equation 72). Thus, it is beneficial that

$$\mathrm{C}(\mathbf{j}) \approx \mathbf{W}_1\mathbf{E}_1\mathbf{W}_1^T \,. \quad (98)$$

Suppose that a two-dimensional orthogonal interpolator (or approximately orthogonal interpolator) is expressible as a family of analytical interpolation functions. Properties of such functions may therefore be adjustable through alteration of the parameters that govern their shape. If this is the case, attainment of interpolator optimality may be possible in the least-squares sense in each modeling context, with function parameters being dependent upon the details of data density, pilot-point density, shape of the model domain, and other factors. Thus, for example, it may be possible to adjust parameters governing $\mathbf{L}$ such that (using equation 97)

$$\mathbf{W}_1\mathbf{E}_1\mathbf{W}_1^T \approx \alpha^2\mathbf{LL}^T\mathbf{WEW}^T\mathbf{LL}^T \,. \quad (99)$$

If $\mathbf{LL}^T$ is orthogonal to $\mathbf{W}_2$ (as ideally it should be—see equation 71), this becomes

$$\mathbf{W}_1 \approx \alpha \mathbf{LL}^T \mathbf{W}_1 . \tag{100}$$

Thus,

$$(\mathbf{I} - \alpha \mathbf{LL}^T)\mathbf{W}_1 = \mathbf{0} . \tag{101}$$

Alternatively (or additionally), the parameters governing L could be adjusted such that the elements of f, defined as

$$\mathbf{W}_2^T \mathbf{L} = \mathbf{f} \tag{102}$$

approach zero in the least-squares sense.

Non-Orthogonal Interpolation

The implicit regularization that attends the use of pilot points was discussed previously. Suppose that an interpolated parameter field is derived from a set of pilot points that are assigned an arbitrary covariance matrix C(**p**). The interpolated parameter field then has the covariance matrix C(**j**) given by

$$C(\mathbf{j}) = \mathbf{L}C(\mathbf{p})\mathbf{L}^T \tag{103}$$

where we do not necessarily assume that **L** represents an orthogonal interpolator.

C(**j**) should possess certain properties. Qualitatively, C(**j**) should resemble C(**k**) as closely as possible up to the nth eigenvector of this matrix, where n is the number of pilot points that are used. (Eigenvectors after the nth are lost through the use of pilot points; hopefully, these lie within the null space of the model operator **Z**.)

To measure the similarity of C(**k**) to C(**j**), we could compute two n-dimensional vectors, which we make as similar to their ideal-valued counterparts as possible in the weighted least-squares sense through adjusting the parameters governing the analytical interpolation functions incorporated in **L**, and maybe the variogram or other analytical stochastic descriptor on which C(**p**) is based.

W contains the first n eigenvectors of C(**k**). A first measure of similarity is that variability of C(**j**) in each of the directions comprising the columns of **W** be the same as that of C(**j**). This occurs if

$$\text{diag}[\mathbf{W}_1^T C(\mathbf{j})\mathbf{W}_1] \approx \text{diag}[\mathbf{E}] \tag{104}$$

where

$$C(\mathbf{k}) = \mathbf{WEW}^T = [\mathbf{W}_1 \quad \mathbf{W}_2]\begin{bmatrix} \mathbf{E}_1 & \mathbf{0} \\ \mathbf{0} & \mathbf{E}_2 \end{bmatrix}\begin{bmatrix} \mathbf{W}_1^T \\ \mathbf{W}_2^T \end{bmatrix} . \tag{105}$$

The second measure of similarity is the alignment of the eigenvectors of C(**j**) with the first n eigenvectors of C(**k**). A high degree of alignment occurs if

$$\sup(\text{row})[\mathbf{W}_1^T \mathbf{U}] \approx 1 \tag{106}$$

where the matrix U holds the eigenvectors of C(**j**), calculated as

$$C(\mathbf{j}) = \mathbf{USU}^T \tag{107}$$

and sup(row) $[\mathbf{W}^T{}_1\mathbf{U}]$ is an n-dimensional vector, the ith element of which is the largest element of the ith row of $\mathbf{W}^T{}_1\mathbf{U}$.

Optimal Emplacement of Pilot Points

When pilot points are dispersed irregularly over a model domain, the locations at which they are placed may exert a considerable influence on their ability to satisfy equations 29 and 64, and thereby to constitute an optimal reduced parameter set. Ideally, emplacement should be at locations within the model domain where the information content of the calibration dataset is most expressed. The focusing of information contained within the calibration dataset is measured by the resolution matrix, this being a by-product of the regularized inversion process. See Menke (1984), Aster and others (2005), and Moore and Doherty (2006) for further details.

To further explain optimal placement of pilot points, a number of synthetic models whose construction is based on a large number of (possibly cell-based) parameters are needed. Resolution matrices for these parameter sets then can be computed based on appropriate synthetic calibration datasets. Computation of derivatives for such large numbers of parameters is most efficiently performed using the adjoint-state formulation of Clemo (written communication, 2007) for MODFLOW-2005. An approximation to the resolution matrix, or the resolution matrix itself, then could be computed based on approximate singular value decomposition as undertaken using the LSQR (Paige and Saunders, 1982) and (or) PROPACK (Larsen, 1998) solvers.

Resolution analyses conducted on such synthetic models would allow a detailed exploration of the effect of placement of pilot points on optimality of the inverse problem solution using a reduced parameter set. In particular, suggestions made in this report that hydraulic conductivity pilot points be placed between head measurement points in the downgradient direction and that storage coefficient pilot points be placed at the same locations as measurement wells, could be evaluated rigorously .

Summary

The following is a list of suggestions for pilot-point use made in this report. These suggestions are based on functionality currently available through parameter-estimation software (PEST) and its utilities along with a current understanding of research and development directions. It is expected that they may be revisited and amended in the future:

1. The number of pilot points used in any particular calibration exercise normally will be limited by practical considerations such as the length of model run times and integrity of finite-difference-based derivatives.

2. In general, use as many pilot points as is numerically practical. In certain modeling contexts, however, a user may wish to limit pilot-point density to limit the spatial frequencies of any heterogeneity that emerges during the calibration process, thereby recognizing that pilot points alone are a type of regularization device.

3. If using Kriging for spatial interpolation, limit the number of pilot points used for interpolation to any cell to a maximum of 10.

4. For some models, it may be possible to use a uniform distribution of pilot points. This may make post-calibration analysis of parameter contributions to current predictive uncertainty easier to interpret. In most cases, however, economy of model runs will dictate that the pilot-point distribution be nonuniform.

5. Use a higher pilot-point density where observation density is greater and a lower pilot-point density elsewhere. Ensure that a minimum pilot-point density prevails throughout the entire model domain, thereby avoiding the occurrence of any "pilot-point deserts."

6. Use an exponential variogram for most cases, and do not specify an excessive variogram range for calculation of Kriging factors; this may lead to local spatial oscillations in the estimated parameter field. If using an exponential variogram the *a* value in the variogram equation should be set to a value that is roughly equal to the maximum distance between any model cell and its closest pilot point if an irregular pilot-point distribution is used. Set it to between one and two times the inter-pilot-point distance if a regular distribution of pilot points is used.

7. Place pilot points at locations at which it is felt that observations are most informative. For pilot points that represent hydraulic conductivity, these locations may lie between observation wells in the direction of groundwater gradient. For pilot points that represent storage properties, pilot points may be best placed directly at observation well locations.

8. Pilot points should be placed at locations where direct measurements of system properties have been made. Regularization equations, and the covariance matrices which govern their application, should be adjusted in accordance with these measurements.

9. Use pervasive Tikhonov regularization. Set the target measurement objective function (PHIMLIM) to a level that is commensurate with that of measurement/structural noise. Be prepared to set it higher during subsequent PEST runs if "overfitting" has resulted in the introduction of geologically unreasonable heterogeneity, indicating that higher-than-expected measurement/structural noise prevails. Alternatively, if the emergence of strong local heterogeneity indicates local model inadequacies, rectify these conceptual inadequacies.

10. Use subspace methods for solution of the inverse problem, regardless of whether Tikhonov regularization is used. Use a Marquardt lambda selection strategy that ensures wide-ranging lambda values.

References Cited

Albert, A., 1972, Regression and the Moore-Penrose Pseudoinverse: New York, Academic Press, 180 p.

Alcolea, A., Carrera, J., and Medina, M., 2006, Inversion of heterogeneous parabolic-type equations using the pilot-points method: International Journal of Numerical Methods in Fluids, v. 51, p. 963–980, doi:10.1002/fld.1213.

Alcolea, A., Carrera, J., and Medina, M., 2008, Regularized pilot-points method for reproducing the effect of small scale variability—Application to simulations of contaminant transport: Journal of Hydrology, v. 335, p. 76–90, doi:10.1016/j.jhydrol.2008.03.004.

Aster, R., Borchers, B., and Thurber, C., 2005, Parameter estimation and inverse problems: Burlington, Mass., Elsevier Academic Press, 301 p.

Cardiff, M., and Kitanidis, P.K., 2009, Bayesian inversion for facies detection—An extensible level set framework: Water Resources Research, v. 45, W10416, 15 p., doi:10.1029/2008wr007675.

Certes, C., and de Marsily, G., 1991, Application of the pilot-points method to the identification of aquifer transmissivities: Advances in Water Resources, v. 14, no. 5, p. 284–300, doi:10.1016/0309-1708(91)90040-U.

Christensen, S., and Doherty, J., 2008, Predictive error dependencies when using pilot-points and singular value decomposition in groundwater model calibration: Advances in Water Resources, v. 31, no. 4, p. 674–700, doi:10.1016/j.advwatres.2008.01.003.

Constable, S.C., Parker, R. L., and Constable C.G., 1987, Occam's inversion—A practical algorithm for generating smooth models from electromagnetic sounding data: Geophysics, v. 52, no. 3, p. 289–300, doi:10.1190/1.1442303.

Cooley, R.L., 2004, A theory for modeling groundwater flow in heterogeneous media: U.S. Geological Survey Professional Paper 1679, 220 p.

De Groot-Hedlin, C., and Constable, S., 1990, Occam inversion to generate smooth, 2-dimensional models from magnetelluric data: Geophysics, v. 55, no. 12, p. 1613–1624, doi:10.1190/1.1442813.

de Marsily, G., Lavedan, C., Boucher, M., and Fasanino, G., 1984, Interpretation of interference tests in a well field using geostatistical techniques to fit the permeability distribution in a reservoir model, *in* Verly, G., David, M., Journel, A.G., and Marechal, A., Geostatistics for natural resources characterization: NATO Advanced Study Institute, ser. C 182, p. 831–849.

Diersch, H.-J. G., 2009, FEFLOW Version 5.4, Finite element subsurface flow and transport simulation system: Berlin, Germany, DHI-WASY GmbH, 202 p.

Doherty, J., 2003, Groundwater model calibration using pilot-points and regularization: Ground Water, v. 41, no. 2, p. 170–177, doi:10.1111/j.1745-6584.2003.tb02580.x.

Doherty, J., 2007, Groundwater data utilities—Part A, Overview: Brisbane, Australia, Watermark Numerical Computing, 67 p.

Doherty, J., 2008, Guidelines for groundwater model calibration using regularized inversion: Brisbane, Australia, Watermark Numerical Computing, 41 p.

Doherty, J., 2010, PEST, Model-independent parameter estimation—User manual (5th ed., with slight additions): Brisbane, Australia, Watermark Numerical Computing.

Doherty, J.E., and Welter, D., 2010, A short explanation of structural noise: Water Resources Research, v. 46, W05525, 14 p., doi: 10.1029/2009wr008377.

Fienen, M.N., Muffels, C.T., and Hunt, R.J., 2009, On constraining pilot point calibration with regularization in PEST: Ground Water, v. 47, no. 6, p. 835–844, doi:10.1111/j.1745-6584.2009.00579.x.

Gallagher, M., and Doherty, J., 2007, Predictive error analysis for a water resource management model: Journal of Hydrology, v. 34, no. 3–4, p. 513–533, doi:10.1016/j.jhydrol.2006.10.037.

Haber, E., 1997, Numerical strategies for the solution of inverse problems: Vancouver, B.C., Canada, University of British Columbia, Department of Geophysics, Ph. D. dissertation, 249 p.

Harbaugh, A.W., 2005, MODFLOW-2005—The U.S. Geological Survey modular ground-water model—The ground-water flow process: U.S. Geological Survey Techniques and Methods book 6, chap. A-16 [variously paged].

Hemker, C.J., and de Boer, R.G., 2009, MicroFEM User's Guide: Amsterdam, The Netherlands, Dr. C.J. (Kick) Hemker, 25 p.

Hill, M.C., and Tiedeman, C.R., 2007, Effective groundwater model calibration—With analysis of data, sensitivities, predictions and uncertainty: Hoboken, N.J., Wiley, 464 p.

Hunt, R.J., and Doherty, J., 2006, A strategy of constructing models to minimize prediction uncertainty, *in* MODFLOW and more 2006—Managing ground water systems, Proceedings of the 7th International Conference of the International Ground Water Modeling Center: Golden, Colo., Colorado School of Mines, p. 56–60.

Hunt, R.J., Doherty, J., and Tonkin, M.J., 2007, Are models too simple?—Arguments for increased parameterization: Ground Water, v. 45, no. 3, p. 254–262, doi:10.1111/j.1745-6584.2007.00316.x.

Hunt, R.J., Luchette, J., Schreuder, W.A., Rumbaugh, J.O., Doherty, J., Tonkin, M.J., and Rumbaugh, D.B., 2010, Using a Cloud to replenish parched groundwater modeling efforts. Rapid Communication for Ground Water 48(3): 360-365, doi: 10.1111/j.1745-6584.2010.00699.x.

Kitanidis, P.K., 1997, Introduction to geostatistics—Applications in hydrogeology: New York, Cambridge University Press, 249 p.

Koch, K.R., 1987, Parameter estimation and hypothesis testing in linear models: Berlin, Springer-Verlag, 333 p.

Kowalsky, M.B., Finsterle S., and Rubin, Y., 2004, Estimating flow parameter distributions using ground-penetrating radar and hydrological measurements during transient flow in the vadose zone: Advances in Water Resources, v. 27, no. 6, p. 583–599, doi:10.1016/j.advwatres.2004.03.003.

Langevin, C.D., Thorne, D.T., Dausman, A.M., Sukop, M.C., and Guo, W., 2008, SEAWAT Version 4—A computer code for simulation of multi-species solute and heat transport: U.S. Geological Survey Techniques and Methods, book 6, chap. A-22, 39 p., accessed March 2, 2010, at http://pubs.usgs.gov/tm/tm6a22/.

Larsen, R.M., 1998, Lanczos bidiagonalization with partial reorthogonalization: Aarhus, Denmark, Aarhus University, Department of Computer Science, Technical report DAIMI PB-357, accessed March 2, 2010, at http://sun.stanford.edu/~rmunk/PROPACK/.

LaVenue, A.M., and Pickens, J.F., 1992, Application of a coupled adjoint sensitivity and Kriging approach to calibrate a groundwater flow model: Water Resources Research, v. 28, no. 6, p. 1543–1569, doi:10.1029/92WR00208.

LaVenue, A.M., RamaRao, B.S., de Marsily, G., and Marietta, M.G., 1995, Pilot-point methodology for automated calibration of an ensemble of conditionally simulated transmissivity fields—2, Application: Water Resources Research, v. 31, no. 3, p. 495–516, doi:10.1029/94WR02259.

LaVenue, M., and de Marsily, G., 2001, Three-dimensional interference test interpretation in a fractured aquifer using the pilot-point inverse method: Water Resources Research, v. 37, no. 11, p. 2659–2675, doi:10.1029/2000WR000289.

Menke, W., 1984, Geophysical data analysis—Discrete inverse theory: New York, Academic Press Inc., 289 p.

Moore, C., and Doherty, J., 2005, The role of the calibration process in reducing model predictive error: Water Resources Research, v. 41, no. 5, W05050.

Moore, C., and Doherty, J., 2006, The cost of uniqueness in groundwater model calibration: Advances in Water Resources, v. 29, no. 4, p. 605–623, doi:10.1016/j.advwatres.2005.07.003.

Moore, E.H., 1920, On the reciprocal of the general algebraic matrix: Bulletin of the American Mathematical Society, v. 26, p. 394–395.

Paige, C.C., and Saunders, M.A., 1982, Algorithm 583—LSQR—Sparse linear equations and least-squares problems: Transactions of Mathematical Software, v. 8, no. 2, p. 195–209.

Parker, R.L., 1977, Understanding inverse theory: Annual Review of Earth and Planetary Sciences, v. 5, no. 1, p. 35–64, doi:10.1146/annurev.ea.05.050177.000343.

Penrose, R., 1955, A generalized inverse for matrices: Mathematical Proceedings of the Cambridge Philosophical Society, v. 51, no. 3, p. 406–413, doi:10.1017/S0305004100030401.

Philip, G.M., and Watson, D.F., 1986, Matheronian geostatistics—Quo Vadis?: Mathematical Geology, v. 18, no. 1, p. 93–117, doi:10.1007/BF00897657.

Portniaguine, O., and Zhdanov M.S., 1999, Focusing geophysical inversion images: Geophysics, v. 64, no. 3, p. 874–887, doi:10.1190/1.1444596.

RamaRao, B.S., LaVenue, A.M., de Marsily, G., and Marietta, M.G., 1995, Pilot-point methodology for automated calibration of an ensemble of conditionally simulated transmissivity fields—1, Theory and computational experiments: Water Resources Research, v. 31, no. 3, p. 475–494, doi:10.1029/94WR02258.

Roberts, M.J., 2004, Signals and systems—Analysis using transform methods and MATLAB: New York, McGraw-Hill, 1072 p.

South Florida Water Management District (SFWMD), 2005, Theory manual—Regional Simulation Model (RSM): West Palm Beach, Fla., SFWMD, Office of Modeling, 308 p.

Tarantola, A., 2005, Inverse problem theory and methods for model parameter estimation: Philadelphia, Pa., Society for Industrial and Applied Mathematics, 358 p

Tikhonov, A.N., 1963a, Solution of incorrectly formulated problems and the regularization method: Soviet Math. Dokl., v. 4, p. 1035–1038.

Tikhonov, A.N., 1963b, Regularization of incorrectly posed problems: Soviet Math. Dokl., v. 4, p. 1624–1627.

Tikhonov, A.N., and Arsenin, V.I.A., 1977, Solution of ill-posed problems: New York, Halsted, 258 p.

Tonkin, M., and Doherty, J., 2005, A hybrid regularized inversion methodology for highly parameterized models: Water Resources Research, v. 41, W10412, doi:10.1029/2005WR003995.

Tonkin, M., and Doherty, J., 2009, Calibration-constrained Monte Carlo analysis of highly-parameterized models using subspace methods: Water Resources Research, v. 45, W00B10, doi:10.1029/2007WR006678.

Tonkin, M., Doherty, J., and Moore, C. 2007, Efficient nonlinear predictive error variance for highly parameterized models. Water Resources Research, v. 43, no. 7, W07429, doi:10.1029/2006WR005348.

Zheng, C., 1990, MT3D—A modular three-dimensional model for simulation of advection, dispersion, and reactions of contaminants in groundwater systems: Ada, Okla., U.S. Environmental Protection Agency, 170 p.

www.ingramcontent.com/pod-product-compliance
Lightning Source LLC
Chambersburg PA
CBHW081800280526
45789CB00008B/2934
* 9 7 8 1 5 0 0 5 0 5 3 4 9 *